Food and Beverage Service Manual

Food and Beverage Service Manual

Matt A. Casado, Ed.D., C.H.A.

John Wiley & Sons, Inc.

New York • Chichester • Brisbane • Toronto • Singapore

Library of Congress Cataloging-in-Publication Data

Casado, Matt A.
    Food and beverage service manual / Matt A. Casado.
      p. cm.
    ISBN 0-471-30464-6 (pbk.)
    1. Table service—United States—Handbooks, manuals, etc.
  2. Wine service—United States—Handbooks, manuals, etc.
  I. Title.
  TX925.C214   1994
  642'.6—dc20
                                           93-43052
                                             CIP

Printed in the United States of America

10 9 8 7 6 5 4 3 2 1

Contents

PART THREE   Cuisine   49

Course Order in Menus   49

Cooking Methods   50

Moist Heat   50
Dry Heat   51

Butters, Thickeners, Flavorings, and Sauces   51

Dish Description   55

Hors d'Oeuvre   56
Appetizers   57
Salads   58
Salad Dressings   58
Soups   59
Eggs and Omelets   63
Seafood   65
Pasta, Dumplings, and Rice   67
Meat and Poultry   68
Vegetables   75
Desserts   78

Culinary Terms   81

PART FOUR   Bar Service   85

Serving Alcoholic Drinks   85

Serving Alcohol and the Law   86

Bar Glassware   86

Types of Alcoholic Beverages   86

Beer   88
Aperitifs   89
Dessert Wines   89
Spirits   90
Liqueurs   92

Preface

This handbook for the service of food and beverages in restaurants is intended for hotel and restaurant waiting personnel and supervisors, bartenders and lounge waiters, wine servers, cooks, and students of hotel and restaurant management schools. It provides clear, concise, and comprehensive guidance in the elements of food and beverage service, service terminology, and the meeting of guest expectations.

Part 1 covers the techniques of table setting and the fundamentals of table service. The various methods of serving food for breakfast, lunch, dinner, banquets, and flaming service are discussed.

Part 2 explains how to serve and suit wines to the different meal courses, and discusses briefly the main wine-producing regions in the United States and Europe.

Part 3 covers methods of cooking, culinary terminology, and menu presentation of dishes from appetizers to desserts. Classic as well as current popular dishes are listed to provide concise, critical information to food service personnel and hospitality students.

Part 4 provides basic knowledge of drinks and bar mixology. It includes a dictionary of classic and popular drinks and a word on liquor regulations.

Much of the book is the result of my expertise as a professional hotelier in the United States and Europe and my teaching experience in one of the leading U.S. schools of hotel and restaurant management, Northern Arizona University. My experience includes training in Switzerland and England, operating hotels and resorts in the United States and Spain, and directing the food and beverage department on cruise ships.

Matt A. Casado, Ed.D., C.H.A.
Northern Arizona University
Flagstaff, Arizona

PART ONE

Food Service

Setting for Service

Before service starts, each service station should be carefully prepared. Tableware, tablecloths, napkins, ashtrays, and serving equipment should be plentiful; condiments, pitchers of iced water, coffee, and roll warmers should also be made ready. In restaurants using cut flowers as decorations, the vases should be washed and refilled with fresh water every day.

Table Setting

For tablecloth service, a silencer cloth generally made of felt should be placed on the table first, attached with clips or with string tied to the table legs. The tablecloth is then placed face up over the silencer cloth with its center crease running along the table's center line. The tablecloth edge should be level with the chair seat or fall at least 12 inches below the table's edge (Fig. 1). A top cloth over the tablecloth, covering just the table's surface, may be used to cover stains. When cloths are changed while meals are in progress, the bare table top should never be allowed to show.

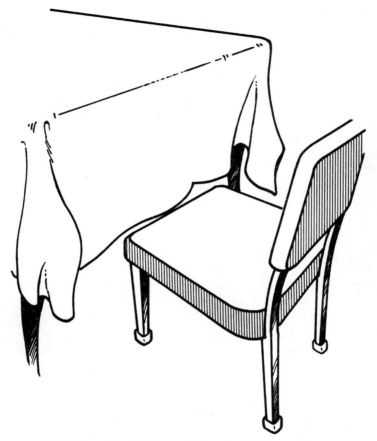

Fig. 1. The tablecloth should be level with the chair's seat.

The napkin should be laid flat or in folds in the center of the cover and one-quarter inch from the table's edge. If the restaurant uses base plates, the napkins should be placed on them. Handling the napkin to create elaborate shapes should be avoided for hygienic reasons. Never set bread on napkins.

Place Setting

A place setting should cover an area of 24 by 15 inches or more. If a base plate is used, the crest or logo should face the guest. When the menu is fixed, as in a banquet, the full place setting should be laid out to suit the menu (Fig. 2). Forks are placed tines up to the left of the napkin, according to the sequence of the dishes to be served, and one-quarter inch from the table's edge. Knives and soup spoons are placed to the right of the napkin, the knife blades facing in. The dessert spoon and fork are placed in front of the napkin, with the fork closest to the napkin and facing right, and the spoon facing left. Fine restaurants add a fish fork and knife when fish is served. The bread and butter plate is placed to the left of the napkin, at least one inch above the fork tines. The butter knife should be placed across the right fourth of the plate, perpendicular to the table's edge, with the blade facing out.

Fig. 2. Banquet place setting with appetizer, soup, entrée, dessert, and two wines.

In restaurants with an à la carte menu, a dinner fork and knife are placed on either side of the napkin (Fig. 3). Additional silverware is brought to the table after the order has been taken, to suit the food ordered.

Water glasses are placed right side up, in line with the tip of the knife (Fig. 3).

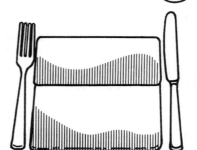

Fig. 3. À la carte place setting with water glass.

Wine glasses are set in order of consumption to the right of the place and toward the center of the table (Fig. 4). Used glasses are removed before the next wine is served, except when guests indicate otherwise.

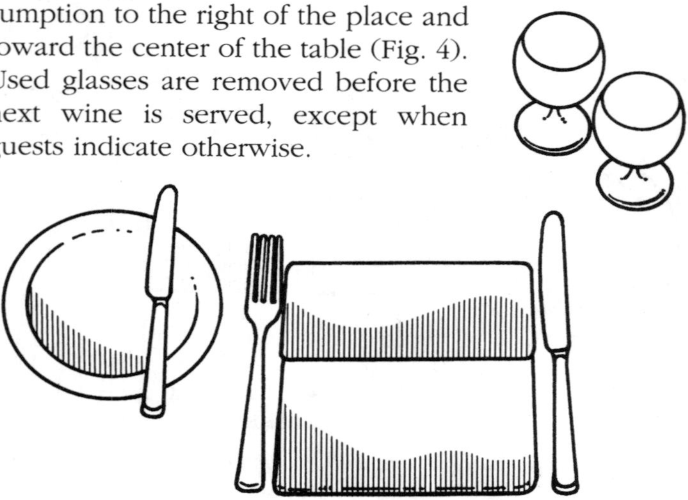

Fig. 4. À la carte place setting with two wines.

Methods of Table Service

European restaurant service follows the old tradition of sumptuous royal banquets. American service is based on efficiency. The names given in Europe to the types of table service differ from country to country. In the United States these names also have different meanings depending on the opinion of restaurant professionals. The descriptions that follow represent the views generally held in the industry.

The method of service offered by a restaurant connotes the degree of formality associated with the establishment. A restaurant should use the type of service best suited to its clientele's desires and needs.

Plate Service (American Service)

The main characteristic of plate service is its pragmatism. It is simple, fast, and efficient, and is by far the most common method of serving food in the United States.

The food is plated in the kitchen, served from the guest's *left* (Fig. 5), and removed from his or her *right*. All beverages are served and cleared from the *right*. Besides being fast, which helps the establishment achieve a high table turnover, this method is labor–cost-effective, as only one server is needed to take care of up to 20 guests efficiently. Another advantage is that it is easily learned by service personnel. The server generally carries the plates from the kitchen to the dining room on a tray, which is placed on a service stand before the guests are served.

Fig. 5. Plate service is from the left.

Cart Service (French Service)

The elegant cart service requires the use of silver service equipment, a side table or cart, and a hot plate or lamp. Two waiters are needed per station: The leading waiter stays in the dining room, giving the guests his total attention; the assistant takes the orders to the kitchen, brings the food and warm plates into the dining room, and helps the leading waiter serve.

The food is carried on silver platters and placed on the side table or cart, where the leading waiter finish-cooks, portions, and places it on warm plates in an appetizing way. The assistant then serves the plates from the guests' *right* (Fig. 6). Plates are removed from the right as well. Vegetables may be offered to the guests separately, going around the table.

The French service is slow, which means a slow table turnover. Also, the restaurant must make more space available for the side tables or carts, and train waiters in tableside cooking. On the other hand, this service is very elegant.

Fig. 6. French service is from the right.

Platter Service (Russian Service)

Russian service is the style most used in first-class restaurants around the world. It is simple, fast, labor–cost-effective, and elegant. The food is fully prepared, portioned, and placed on silver serving platters in the kitchen. Using a tray, the waiter brings the platters and warm plates to the dining room and places them on a tray stand or service table. Before beginning service, the waiter presents the silver platter to the table host, and then sets the warm plates before the guests from the guests' *right*, going around the table counter-clockwise. Holding the platter in his or her left hand with a folded napkin underneath, the waiter serves the guests from their *left* (Fig. 7). The platter should be held so that its

Fig. 7. Platter service.

edge is slightly above the plate (Fig. 7) The food is served from the platter onto the plates with a serving fork and spoon (Fig. 8).

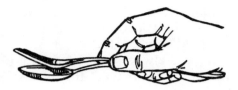

Fig. 8. In platter service, food is transferred to the guest's plate with a serving fork and spoon.

For small parties, the main course and garnish can be placed on the same platter. For large parties, the main course is served from the platter and the garnish (starch and vegetables) and gravies are served from separate silver bowls.

Russian service can be performed by one waiter per station. However, the waiter needs to be specially trained. Restaurant operators who want to offer this elegant service must make a substantial investment in silverware. On the other hand, silverware is very durable.

Restaurant Service

The essence of service is anticipation of the guest's needs. Simply coming to the table several times to ask if "everything is all right" is not enough.

The server should be quiet and quick, and should never intrude on the guest. Service personnel should recognize the thin line between "friendliness" and "familiarity" and be careful not to cross it.

Dining room personnel should always be neatly dressed and groomed and must avoid the use of cigarettes and chewing gum while on duty. Waiting personnel should be alert, hold themselves straight, and keep their hands and nails very clean. Their shoes must be polished, and they must be prepared for frequent changes of shirts and socks. A clean, unstained service cloth, carried on the left forearm, should be used (Fig. 9).

Silverware should always be carried on a plate, tray, or napkin, never by hand (Fig. 10). Plates should be held by the edge to avoid finger marks (Fig. 11). When

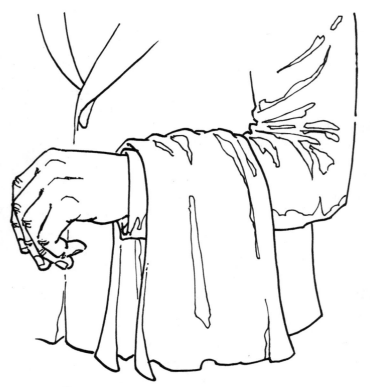

Fig. 9. A service cloth is carried on the left arm.

Fig. 10. Silverware carried on a plate and handled by the stem.

Fig. 11. Plates are held at the very edge by the fingers.

plate covers are used, they are to be placed upside down on the service table. Glasses should be carried and handled by the base or stem, never grasped by the rim, even when soiled (Fig. 12). Hot plates are carried and handled using the service cloth (Fig. 13).

Service personnel must never lean on the table or chairs. Running in restaurants is out of the question. Guests should never be hurried.

Fig. 12. Glasses are handled by the base or stem.

Fig. 13. Hot plates are carried with the service cloth.

In most American restaurants:

- Food is served from the *left*.
- Beverages are served from the *right*.
- Dishes and glasses are cleared from the *right*.

FINGER BOWLS: Finger bowls are served with (not after) foods that guests eat with their fingers, such as game fowl (quail, partridge, pheasant, grouse), shellfish (lobster, crayfish, prawns), mollusks (mussels, oysters, clams), some vegetables (boiled artichokes, corn on the cob, asparagus), frogs' legs, and fresh unpeeled fruit. One bowl should be placed in front of the plate, on a saucer or dessert plate covered with a doily or folded napkin (Fig. 14). It should be half-filled with cold or warm water, depending on whether cold or hot dishes are served. A lemon slice or a flower petal may be added to the water for decoration.

Fig. 14. A finger bowl is placed in front of the place setting.

MUSTARD: Mustard is brought to the table when cold meats, processed pork meat, ham, and all types of sausage are served.

GRATED CHEESE: Grated cheese should be served with pasta dishes, minestrone and onion soups, and risotto.

WASTE PLATE: A dessert-size plate should be placed on the table when foods with inedible parts, such as boiled artichokes, bone-in fish, lobster, and shellfish, are served.

The Psychology of Service

Different guests require different serving approaches. It is up to the waiter to identify the needs of the people to be served. While the quality of the food and the restaurant atmosphere are very important, the right type of service for each guest in each circumstance is critical. For instance:

- The guest in a hurry requires, above all, speedy service.
- Solo guests generally appreciate some conversation.
- Some guests welcome less expensive menu suggestions.
- Guests engaged in animated conversation should not be unnecessarily interrupted.
- Regular guests appreciate being seated at their "usual" tables.
- Guests who expect special recognition should be accorded extra attention.
- Some guests need help with their menu selections; others might be irritated if the waiter insists on explaining the bill of fare.

Welcoming the Guest

Guests entering a restaurant should always be approached immediately by someone on the restaurant staff and cordially greeted. Make eye contact. When possible, offer a choice of table. For instance, say "Would you like a seat by the window or do you prefer a booth?" The waiter or other staff member precedes the guest to the table, being careful not to walk too briskly. It is correct to sit the women facing the dining room rather than the wall. When the guest approaches the table, the chair should be held for him or her. Unneeded setups should be removed from the table at this time.

Menus

Service personnel should know the menu by heart, be aware of how long it takes to prepare each dish, and be familiar with the specials offered that day. There must be very good communication between the chef and the dining room manager, who should speak to the waiters before service starts about dishes to be specially recommended.

Menus should be carried by hand, never under the arm, and handed to women first. Women, older guests, and children are served first; the table host is served last.

Taking Orders

Serving personnel must accommodate the needs of both guest and restaurant. They should sense the type of meal guests are looking for: copious, light, healthy, diet, inexpensive, or fancy, yet be courteous and subtle in their suggestions. Guests, in general, abhor restaurants with "pushy" service personnel.

Each order is taken from the guest's left. The waiter first asks the person to the right of the table host and continues counter-clockwise, unless the host decides to order for everybody. In order to eliminate confusion at the time of serving, the waiter should mentally assign the number 1 to a chair at each table and take the order in a set pattern (Fig. 15).

Cocktail orders are taken and served first, before food orders. Suggest appetizers. The wine order is taken immediately after the food order. With hosted parties, the wine list should be presented to the host only, unless he or she indicates otherwise. Orders for dessert are taken after all guests have finished eating the main course and the plates have been cleared.

Because dishes have different preparation times, servers should know in advance how long it takes to prepare each item on the menu. Orders to the kitchen should be

An abbreviation system for taking orders

Table 15		
1 S	FM r	C. bp
2 Sc	R m	Cf, ff
3 S	FM w	Cf, ff
4 S	F	B, bp
5 LC	F	B, bp

Sc	Shrimp Cocktail	**m**	medium
LC	Lobster Cocktail	**w**	well done
S	Soup	**C**	Carrots
FM	Filet Mignon	**Cf**	Cauliflower
R	Roast Beef	**B**	Beans
F	Fish	**bp**	boiled potatoes
r	rare	**ff**	french fried potatoes

Fig. 15. Guest orders are taken in a set pattern.

placed sequentially so that dishes can be served to guests at the same time. If guests order dishes that require substantially different preparation times, they should be so informed. The server should keep his or her attention on the guests at all times, anticipating needs and checking whether a guest is trying to communicate.

Carrying Trays

Large trays are carried on the left hand, above the shoulder, balanced on the palm or the fingertips (Fig. 16).

Fig. 16. Light trays can be balanced on the fingertips.

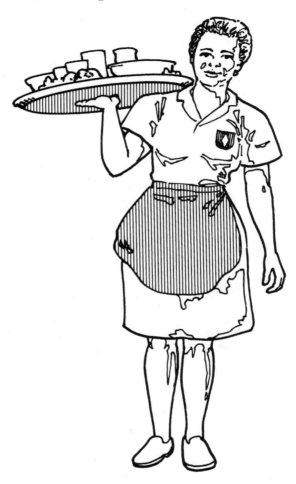

Fig. 17. Heavy trays can rest on the shoulder.

Very heavy trays can rest on the shoulder (Fig. 17). Tall bottles should not be carried on trays. Small, light trays should be carried waist high (Fig. 18).

Fig. 18. Small, light trays can be carried waist high.

Clearing the Table

A course should be cleared from the table when all guests have finished eating. Dirty glasses should be carried away on a tray; empty bottles should be carried by hand. Before dessert is served, all dishes, glasses, and condiments should be cleared from the table except for the coffee service and water goblets. Crumbs should be brushed from the table with a folded napkin or brush.

Presenting the Bill

The bill should be presented to the guest folded or face down on a tray or small plate. The waiter should not stand beside a guest while he or she is inspecting the bill. Customers staying at the hotel should be asked to sign their bills and write their room numbers on them. Bills should be posted to their accounts immediately.

The waiter should thank the guest graciously for any tip. The restaurant manager, host, or waiter should be present when the guest leaves, inviting him or her to come again.

Accidents in the Dining Room

If food is spilled on the table, the waiter should brush it onto a plate, clean the spot with a damp cloth, and cover it with a clean napkin. If food is spilled on the carpet in view of guests, it should be immediately covered with a white napkin to prevent anyone from stepping on it, and then quickly removed.

If food is spilled on a guest, the guest should be asked to go to the restaurant office for prompt attention to the problem.

Breakfast Service

Today's busy traveler and vacationer expect breakfast service to be on time and fast. Product freshness is also expected. Operators should strive to offer coffee, pastries, toast, juices, and cooked items as freshly prepared as possible.

Place Setting

For continental breakfast, a dessert plate, small napkin, small knife, and saucer with a teaspoon should be pre-set (Fig. 19). The cup should be kept warm and brought to the table when beverages are served. Beverages can be served from a tray, or they can be served by the waiter, who places a folded napkin just under the spout of the pot or decanter. Hot chocolate jugs should be placed on a saucer to avoid soiling the tablecloth. When individual tea or coffee pots are used, they should be placed to the right and slightly to the front of the cup. Rolls, toast, butter, and jams should be positioned in front of the guest.

Fig. 19. Continental breakfast place setting.

For full, or English, breakfast, additional cutlery must be added to the place setting (Fig. 20).

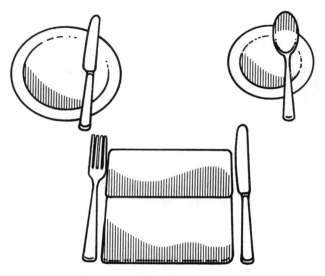

Fig. 20. Full breakfast place setting.

Room Service

Like breakfast served in the dining room, room-service breakfast must be served on time. Sufficient one- and two-guest trays should be prepared in advance of service (Figs. 21, 22, 23). Each tray should be covered with a placemat or napkin, and all the silverware and crockery should be laid out except for the cup, which must be kept warm. When orders are taken the evening before for a specific hour, allow for the time it takes to prepare the various items. Plates with cooked items must be covered with a plate cover.

Trays should be carried on the left hand. Knock firmly on the guest's door, announcing "room service," and

Fig. 21. Tray set for continental breakfast for one guest.

Fig. 22. Tray set for continental breakfast for two guests.

Fig. 23. Tray set for continental breakfast for three guests.

wait for a reply before entering. Come back to the room after a reasonable time to remove the tray. All trays placed by guests in corridors should be cleared before the end of the shift.

Banquet Service

Exact information about a banquet is a prerequisite for efficient banquet service. The restaurant or banquet manager should know ahead of time the approximate number of people attending, the sitting structure, the menu to be served, and the time the banquet will begin.

Table Setting

Restaurants offering banquet service should have sectional tables to form the different table arrangements required for large numbers of people (Figs. 24, 25). Tablecloths

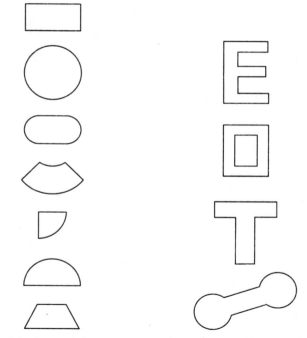

Fig. 24. Common banquet table shapes.

Fig. 25. Common banquet table arrangements.

should be laid with the main crease in the center of the table, extending over the edge to the level of the chair seats.

Place Setting

Napkins are placed at equal distances. All silverware, crockery, and glassware needed to serve all courses should be polished and set in advance, as described in the section on place setting for restaurant service. Salt and pepper shakers are placed between every four or five places.

Service Protocol

The shape of the table should conform to the organizer's requirements. The seat of honor is to the right of the host; the second seat of honor is to the left. Additional seats of honor should be assigned following this sequence.

Welcoming the Host

The banquet manager should contact the banquet organizer or host to offer any assistance or receive any special instructions or changes before the banquet begins.

Types of Banquet Service

Two types of service are commonly used in banquets: plate, or American, and platter, or Russian. In American service, the food is plated in the kitchen, topped with plate covers, and carried to the banquet room on trays. The service proceeds as described in the section on American service.

In Russian service, the food is portioned in the kitchen and brought into the banquet room on silver platters holding 6 to 10 portions each. A warm plate is placed in front of each guest, from the guest's right, and the food is served by the waiter from the guest's *left*. Vegetables and gravies are usually served by a second waiter after the main course has been served. This service is elegant and saves plating time in the kitchen.

In Russian service, all waiters should enter the banquet room at the same time, carrying the platters. Service should start simultaneously, beginning slightly ahead with the head table. The clearing of plates should also start simultaneously.

Flambé Service

Fine restaurants often feature flaming dishes. At banquets, flaming desserts provide an opportunity for spectacular displays of showmanship.

For flaming dishes, a cart with one or two propane burners is generally used (Fig. 26). Flaming can also be

Fig. 26. Two-burner flaming cart.

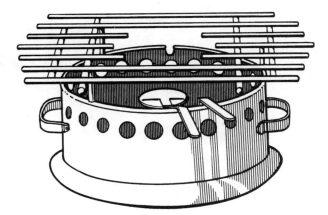

Fig. 27. Flaming lamp.

done on a side table using a lamp fueled with alcohol or sterno (Fig. 27). The food to be flamed is totally or partially prepared in the kitchen and brought to tableside, where the waiter flames it in a sauté pan using spirits or liqueurs (Fig. 28). After the dish has been flamed, the food is placed on warm plates and served.

The flaming of entrées, desserts, and drinks requires a restaurant captain or trained waiters. If flaming is to be performed by waiters in charge of stations, the number of guests to be served per station should be reduced to 10 or 12.

Fig. 28. Flaming sauté pan.

PART TWO

Wine Service

Wine is the beverage that results from the fermentation of crushed grapes. The fermentation takes place in vats, where yeast converts the sugar in the grape juice to alcohol and carbon dioxide. Drinking wine with meals is a tradition in Europe and is becoming a trend in America. Because the cost of having wine with lunch or dinner substantially raises the total of the bill, wines should be moderately priced.

The proper storing of wines is essential to maintain their quality, as light and the wrong temperature will cause them to deteriorate. The main storage, or cellar, should be kept between 50 and 60 F. Wine bottles should always be stored horizontally so that air does not sit between the wine and the cork.

Types of Wines

Dry wines are produced by allowing fermentation to last until most of the grape sugar is turned into alcohol. If fermentation is stopped early, much sugar remains and the wine that results is known as *sweet. Light* wines contain relatively little alcohol, from 7 to 12 percent, while *robust* wines such as ports and sherries contain from 15 to 20 percent. A *still* wine is one in which the carbon dioxide generated during fermentation has been allowed to escape before bottling. A *sparkling* wine is bottled before the fermentation is complete, so that the carbon dioxide remains in it. A *fortified* wine contains added brandy or other spirits and is marketed as an *aperitif,* such as vermouth, and *dessert wine,* such as port.

White Wines

White wine is made from the juice of white grapes or from the juice of black or pink grapes from which the skins, which contain the coloring, have been removed. White wines can be very dry or very sweet, and in general they are more delicate than reds.

Red Wines

Red wine is made from the juice of black grapes that are allowed to ferment along with their skins. Most red wines are aged in oakwood casks for over six months, where they mellow and acquire their characteristic flavor.

Rosé Wines

The making of rosé wines is similar to the making of reds, except that the fermentation period is reduced to one or two days—enough to give the wine its pink color. Rosés need only a couple of months to mature before bottling.

Sparkling Wines

To make a sparkling wine, or champagne, additional sugar and yeast are added to a still wine to cause a second fermentation. This time, the carbon dioxide is not allowed to escape but is retained in the wine. The amount of added sugar determines the relative dryness of the champagne. Common types of champagne are:

Brut, or very, very dry
Extra dry, or fairly dry
Dry, or sweet
Demi-sec, or quite sweet
Doux, or very sweet

House Wines

House wines are generally generic wines of broad denomination. Restaurants and bars serve house wines with the generic names of *chablis* for white and *burgundy* for red. These wines are often bought in large bottles or jugs and sold by the glass or in decanters.

Dessert Wines

Dessert wines are sweet, still wines that have been fortified with extra alcohol, generally brandy. They are rich and heavy, appropriate for serving after meals. These wines are very good for cooking, as they add much taste and richness to meats and seafood. Some dessert wines are sherry, Madeira, port, and Marsala.

Serving Wines

Wine glasses are always placed to the right of the water glass. When two or more wines are to be served, the glasses are arranged so that the first wine will be at the right. Each glass is removed before the next wine is served. Wine glasses are carried on small trays or upside down with the stem between the fingers. The rim of the glass must never be touched.

Wine Temperatures

White, rosé, and sparkling wines are served chilled but not iced. A small stock needed for about a week's service should be kept under refrigeration and available for prompt service.

Red wines should be served at room temperature. A small stock should be kept in the area in which it is to be served, or at room temperature. It is out of the question to place wines in freezers to chill them or in hot water or on a hot plate to warm them up. The sudden temperature change will destroy their quality.

As a rule, serve:

Sparkling wines: very cold, 40–45 F
White and rosé wines: cold, 45–55 F
Red wines: room temperature, 60–68 F

How to Open a Bottle

The best corkscrew is the flat jackknife type with lever and blade (Fig. 29). The first step in opening is to cut the foil well below the lip of the bottle using the blade

Fig. 29. Corkscrew.

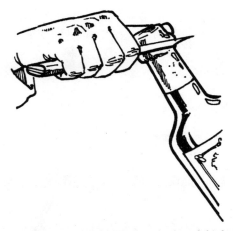

Fig. 30. Cut the foil well below the lip of the bottle.

(Fig. 30). Never rip the capsule off with the fingernail. If there is a bit of mold at the top of the cork, wipe it with a clean napkin (Fig. 31). Then insert the worm of the corkscrew in the middle of the cork and turn carefully, straight down, with moderate pressure. Next, place the lever in position, holding the bottle firmly

Fig. 31. Wipe the mouth.

with the left hand, and carefully remove the cork. Take care not to shake the bottle (Fig. 32). Finally, wipe the

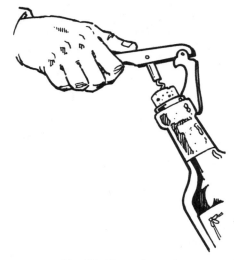

Fig. 32. Draw the cork.

lip of the bottle with the clean napkin and present the cork to the host (Fig. 33).

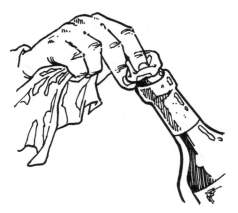

Fig. 33. Wipe again.

Sparkling wine bottles have mushroom-shaped corks secured by a wire hood. First, remove the foil by hand, and then, keeping a thumb over the cork, remove the safety wire by untwisting the wireloop on the bottle neck. Keeping the bottle at a 45-degree angle, grasp the cork firmly and twist the bottle, or hold the bottle and twist the cork, pulling it out. Champagne should be uncorked with a minimum of noise and served immediately. If there is gushing after the bottle is opened, pour some quickly and the gushing will stop (Fig. 34).

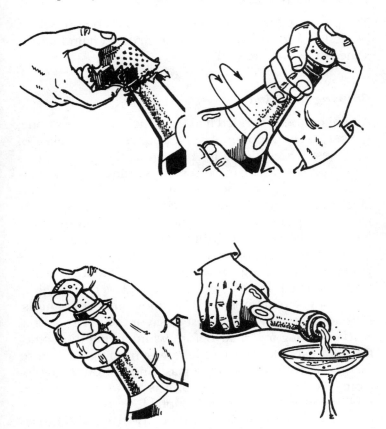

Fig. 34. Opening a champagne bottle.

Wine Service

Bottled wine should be opened at the table, in full view
of the guest who ordered it. Aged red wines should be
carried very carefully, preferably in a bottle basket, with
the label up. After the wine has been ordered, it should
be served at the beginning of the meal, unless the guest
wishes to have it served with the main course.

Presenting the Wine

The person who ordered the wine should be shown the
bottle label so that he or she can make certain that the
wine is the one ordered.

Pouring the Wine

After it has been verified that the wine is the correct one,
the server should pour about an ounce into the glass of
the guest who ordered it. As soon as the guest signals
approval, the wine can be served, starting with the person to the right of the host and proceeding counter-
clockwise, filling the host's glass last. Wine is served
from the right of the guest, the bottle held in the right
hand, by the body, with the label facing upward. The
server should not pour wine by passing the bottle across
guests or by serving the entire table without changing
position. The bottle is brought to the glass on the table.

Glasses should not be filled more than two-thirds.
This amount allows the guest to savor the wine's aroma
before starting to drink. Before withdrawing the bottle,
the server should give it a slight twist from right to left so
that the last drop falls in the glass and not on the tablecloth. As the meal progresses, it is up to the server to
refill the glasses as they are emptied.

Figure 35 illustrates the various types of wine glass
and describes their use with different wines.

All Purpose.
Used for reds or
whites.

All Purpose.
Good for reds,
rosés, and hearty
whites.

Rhine Wine.
Used for light
whites.

Dessert Wine.
Used for ports,
Tokay, and other
dessert wines, or
sweet sherries.

Sherry.
Used for dry or
cocktail sherries.

**Champagne
Saucer.**
Used for sparkling
wines.

Champagne Tulip.

Used for sparkling wines.

Fig. 35. Types of wine glass.

White wines are brought to the table in an ice bucket draped with a clean folded napkin. The ice bucket should be placed on a stand to the right of the person who ordered the wine. If the bucket is to be placed on the table, a plate should be put under it to prevent the tablecloth from getting wet.

White wine is poured from a couple of inches above the glass unless it is aged; in that case, the bottle should almost touch the glass.

As red wines grow older, they develop sediment at the bottom of the bottle. For this reason, they are to be handled very gently. Wine baskets help transport mature red wines without disturbing the sediment. Red wine is to be poured very delicately, with the bottle almost in contact with the rim of the glass. After the glasses are filled, the bottle is placed at the right of the host.

Like white wines, sparkling wines are placed in an ice bucket for serving. The wine should be poured in two motions: The first one will fill the glass with froth; the second, when the froth subsides, will fill the glass about two-thirds full.

The Wine List

The wine list should complement the menu and be in line with the type of operation in which it is being used. A steak house, for instance, must have a good selection of red wine, while a seafood restaurant should feature mainly white. The service staff should know how the wines on the list taste, how their names are pronounced, and which best suit each of the courses of the menu. The wine list should be presented to the host just before the food is ordered. It is a good idea to identify each wine with a number to spare the guest having to pronounce its name.

Servers should become familiar with the terms on the

wine list that describe the characteristics of wines. The most common are these:

Body: the feel of the wine in the mouth. A full-bodied wine will cling to the side of the glass if it is swished around; a light-bodied wine will not.

Bouquet: the scent of the wine.

Character: the distinct taste.

Dry: in white wine, low in sugar.

Flat: lacking in body.

Fruity: tasting of grape.

Generous: having substantial alcohol content.

Light: having moderate alcohol content.

Mellow: aged, not too sweet.

Robust: having a high alcohol content.

Sweet: in white wine, rich in sugar.

Which Wine with Which Food?

Matching a wine with a dish is the guest's prerogative; however, servers should be very familiar with the wines that best suit the courses of a meal. They should know, for instance, that a strongly flavored dish is served with a robust wine, while a delicate entrée is served with a light one. White precedes red when more than one wine is served; light is served before robust; new before aged; and dry before sweet. If a guest asks a server to recommend a wine with the meal, the following suggestions are in order:

Appetizer: a light, dry white.

Soup or salad: no wine or the wine that will be served after these starters.

Seafood: a dry or medium white.

Veal, pork, or poultry: a light red, a dry full-bodied white, or a rosé.

Red meat or game: a robust red.

Pasta: a full-bodied red.

Desserts: a sparkling wine, a sweet white, or a dessert wine.

When recommending wines, the waiter should be careful not to push only the most expensive choices but to offer the guest a few alternatives within an expensive/inexpensive range. If two guests are eating together and one orders meat and the other fish, a rosé wine is appropriate as it goes well with either. Ultimately, the choice of wine rests with the guest. There is nothing wrong with serving white wine with red meat if the guest so desires. In any case, the wine ordered should be served without comment.

Wine-Producing Regions

For centuries, the production of wines was a monopoly of the nations of central and southern Europe: France, Spain, Italy, Greece, Portugal, and, to a lesser extent, Germany. Today, the United States as well is a significant producer of very good and plentiful wines. This increase in U.S. production has followed a substantial increase in consumption; while some years ago few Americans drank wine, today wine sales have outpaced the sale of spirits.

FRANCE

Fig. 36. French wine regions.

France

The climate and soil of French wine-producing regions are perfect for the cultivation of grapes. The quality of wines exported by France is almost always very good. Although most French areas produce wines, these are most famous (Fig. 36):

ALSACE: The wines produced in Alsace are mostly white. They are generally dry, mellow, light, and of strong, fruity bouquet. Alsatian wines can be recommended for seafood and poultry. Good ones are **Riesling, Gewurztraminer, Sylvaner,** and **Tokay.**

BORDEAUX: The French southwestern region of Bordeaux is the origin of the most prestigious wines in France. Although the area produces good white wines, the term *Bordeaux* connotes red. The British call the red wines from Bordeaux **clarets.**

Often, the word *château,* or *castle,* is used to designate the vineyard the wine comes from. Bordeaux red wines must be recommended to accompany a red meat entrée, such as roast beef. Some of these wines are aged for up to 20 years before they are put on the market. For the most part, Bordeaux wines are light, ruby-red, and very delicate.

The white wines grown in the Bordeaux district of Graves are dry, while those produced in the district of Sauternes are mellow and sweet. Some of the famous wine-growing areas of Bordeaux are **Médoc, Graves, Sauternes, Saint-Émilion, Saint-Julien, Margaux, Barsac,** and **Entre-Deux-Mers.** Some of the better-known wines are **Château Lafite-Rothschild, Château Margaux, Château Latour, Château Mouton Rothschild,** and **Château d'Yquem.**

BURGUNDY: Wines produced in Burgundy are second in fame to those of Bordeaux. The region produces good reds and whites. The red wines are generally light, fresh, and fruity and go very well with red meats, particularly wild game. The best known wine-growing districts are **Chablis, Côte de Nuits, Beaujolais, Côte de Beaune,** and **Côte Mâconnaise.** Famous wines from this area are **Vosne-Romanée, Nuits-Saint-George, Aloxe-Corton, Meursault, Puilly Fuissé,** and **Moulin-à-Vent.**

CHAMPAGNE: Champagne is the northeast corner of France, famous for its sparkling wines. Champagne can be recommended with appetizers and desserts. Some of the well-known labels are **Möet et Chandon, Mercier, Veuve Clicquot, Pommery et Greno, Mumm,** and **Taittinger.**

Germany

German wines come from regions along the Rhine and Moselle rivers and are generally white and young. Moselle wines are light and dry, while those from the Rhine region are robust. German wines can be recommended with seafood and veal dishes. Germany also produces champagne-like wines called *sekt*. The best known wine-producing regions are **Piesport, Zell, Rheingau, Nierstein, Rheinhessen,** and **Pfalz** (Fig. 37).

GERMANY

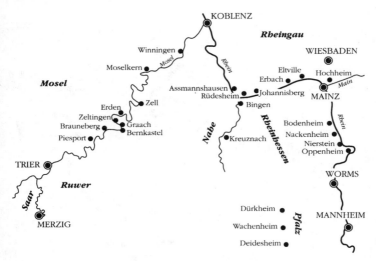

Fig. 37. German wine regions.

Italy

Italy has been producing wines since the time of the Romans. Today, it produces many wines that are generally strong and bouqueted. Red Italian wines are a necessary complement for pasta dishes, while whites go very well with poultry and white meat. Well-known table wines from Italy are **Barbera, Barolo, Asti Spumante, Chianti, Frascati, Orvieto,** and **Marsala** (Fig. 38).

ITALY

Fig. 38. Italian wine regions.

United States

The quality of American wines has improved so much in the last two decades that they can now be compared to those of France and Germany. While the number of wine-producing regions is rapidly expanding, California is the best known, for its quality and quantity. Reds, whites, rosés, and sparkling wines of excellent quality are available to the American and overseas consumer at very reasonable prices. The main producing California regions are **North Bay, South Bay, Great Valley,** and **Los Angeles** (Fig. 39).

CALIFORNIA

Fig. 39. California wine regions.

California wines take their names from the predominant grapes they are made from. Following are the most common varietal names.

WHITES:

Chardonnay: aged in oak barrels, it goes very well with seafood served with cream sauces.

Chenin Blanc: rather sweet, this light, fruity wine can be recommended to go with shellfish and poultry.

Fume Blanc: dry, with a distinct smoky flavor, it goes very well with seasoned poultry dishes.

Gewurztraminer: very spicy, making it go well with appetizers such as pâté.

Johannisberger Riesling: fruity in flavor and very good with shellfish.

Sylvaner: clean and fruity, with a tinge of sweetness; it goes well with seafood and poultry dishes.

REDS:

Cabernet Sauvignon: a prestigious dry, full-bodied red; when aged, it is a must with beef and lamb dishes.

Gamay: light, fresh, and fruity; it can be recommended to go with pork dishes.

Merlot: similar to Cabernet Sauvignon, but softer in character; it goes very well with red meats.

Petite Sirah: dry and robust; it is well suited to complement seasoned meats.

Pinot Noir: dry but delicate; it is a favored wine with beef dishes.

Zinfandel: a delicate, fresh wine that goes well with veal and pork dishes; its flavor brings berries to mind.

PART THREE

Cuisine

Course Order in Menus

Restaurants offer foods listed as courses, or groups of dishes. Guests generally select one item from each group. Most menus offer three or more courses, which are listed in order of service. The traditional order of serving foods is as follows:

Appetizers	before
Soups	before
Fish	before
Meat	before
Desserts	before
Cheese	

Salads may be served before the main dish, with it, or after it. Listed below are examples of meals with different courses:

One-course   main dish
Two-course   appetizer, soup or salad/main dish

or

main dish/dessert

Three-course	appetizer, soup or salad/main dish/ dessert
Four-course	appetizer, soup or salad and/or fish/ main dish/dessert
Five-course	appetizer/soup or salad/fish/main dish (not seafood)/dessert

Cooking Methods

Service personnel must be familiar with the ways food is prepared and be able to describe these ways to guests.

Moist Heat

Moist-heat cooking is the preparation of food in steam, water, or water-based liquids. Items prepared this way are leaner than if cooked in fat and therefore may be recommended to health-conscious guests. The following are moist-heat cooking methods commonly found on restaurant menus.

Boiled: cooked in liquid at 212 F.

Braised: stewed in a small amount of liquid in a covered container, over a low fire or in a moderate oven.

en Papillote: cooked wrapped in parchment paper or aluminum foil.

Poached: gently cooked in liquid at about 170 F.

Simmered: cooked in liquid just below a boil.

Steamed: cooked surrounded by a vapor bath.

Dry Heat

Dry-heat cooking transfers heat without using water or steam. Cooking with fats and oils is considered a dry-heat method. Dishes prepared with any type of grease are generally high in calories. Foods cooked by the dry-heat method are featured on menus with the following descriptions.

Baked: cooked by heated air in an oven.

Broiled: cooked by direct heat radiating from above.

Fried: cooked in hot fat.

Deep-Fried: cooked submerged in hot fat.

Grilled: cooked on a grate by direct heat radiating from below.

Roasted: cooked in the oven or on a revolving spit.

Sautéed: cooked in a small amount of fat over high heat.

Stir-Fried: cut in small pieces and sautéed over high heat while the pan is flipped quickly.

Butters, Thickeners, Flavorings, and Sauces

Very often, dishes are given the name of the butter or sauce with which they are served. Service personnel must be able to recognize and explain the composition of these additives.

BUTTERS:

Black: cooked to a very dark brown.

Café de Paris: mixed with garlic, anchovy, parsley, chives, eggs, Madeira, and brandy.

Colbert: maître d'hôtel butter with meat glaze and tarragon.

Escargot: mixed with crushed garlic, chopped parsley, and white pepper.

Maître d'Hôtel: cold butter mixed with chopped parsley, lemon juice, and white pepper.

Meunière: noisette butter seasoned with lemon juice and chopped parsley.

Noisette: heated to a golden-brown color.

THICKENERS:

Liaison: a mixture of egg yolks and cream.

Manié Butter: raw butter kneaded with an equal part of flour.

Roux: one part cooked fat to one part flour. The length of cooking will determine if a roux will be white, golden, or brown.

FLAVORINGS:

Bouquet Garni: a small bundle of herbs, usually parsley, bay leaf, and thyme, used to flavor stocks and braised dishes.

Duxelle: a mixture of finely chopped mushrooms and shallots sautéed in butter.

Matignon: an addition to poêlé dishes of carrots, celery, leeks, and onions.

Mirepoix: an addition to stocks, soups, or stews of chopped vegetables such as carrots, onions, and celery.

Persillade: a mixture of minced parsley, garlic, and bread crumbs.

Pesto: a mixture of olive oil, basil, and seasonings commonly used for pasta.

SAUCES: There are six basic sauces from which most others are made. It is important for servers to be familiar with these leading sauces.

Demi-Glace: a rich brown sauce.

Velouté: veal, poultry, or fish white stock thickened with roux.

Béchamel: a white sauce made by diluting roux with milk.

Tomato: tomatoes and stock flavored with bacon, vegetables, and herbs.

Hollandaise: an emulsion of egg yolks and clarified butter with fresh lemon juice.

Mayonnaise: a cold sauce of egg yolks, oil, vinegar, and mustard.

SECONDARY SAUCES: Here are the basic ingredients of a selection of classic and contemporary secondary sauces:

Aïoli: mayonnaise with added crushed garlic.

Albufera: a poultry velouté with added cream and meat glaze.

Allemande: a veal or chicken velouté thickened with egg yolks and cream.

Aurora: a velouté colored with tomato puree.

Béarnaise: a reduction of egg yolks and melted butter with shallots, vinegar, and tarragon.

Bigarade: a reduction of red wine, orange juice, and orange and lemon peel strips with demi-glace.

Bordelaise: a reduction of red wine, shallots, and herbs with demi-glace.

Cardinal: a béchamel with fish stock and lobster butter.

Chasseur: a demi-glace with chopped mushrooms.

Chaud-Froid: a demi-glace with meat or fish gelatin.

Choron: a béarnaise with tomato purée.

Coulis: a puree of a vegetable, generally red pepper, broccoli, or tomato, with sautéed onions and cream and/or butter.

Cumberland: red currant jelly with port wine, mustard, and shredded orange and lemon peel.

Dill: a velouté with lightly sautéed onions, cream, and chopped dill.

Dugleré: a fish velouté with crushed tomatoes.

Foyot: a béarnaise with added meat glaze.

Grand Veneur: a pepper sauce thickened with blood from the meat the sauce will be served with.

Hungarian: a white wine velouté with onions and paprika.

Jus Lié: a stock thickened with arrowroot or cornstarch.

Maltaise: a hollandaise with orange juice and shredded peel.

Marchand de Vin: a reduction of red wine and shallots with meat glaze.

Matelote: a reduction of red wine, fish stock, and mushrooms.

Mornay: a béchamel with grated Parmesan cheese.

Mousseline: a hollandaise with cream.

Nantua: a fish velouté with tomato and shrimp butter.

Normandy: a fish velouté with mushrooms.

Paprika: a veal velouté with onion, paprika, and cream.

Périgueux: a demi-glace with Madeira wine and truffles.

Poivrade: a reduction of shallots, vinegar, and pepper-corns, thinned with demi-glace and game stock.

Portugaise: a tomato sauce with onions, garlic, and crushed tomatoes.

Poulette: a mushroom velouté.

Rémoulade: mayonnaise with capers, gherkins, and chopped anchovies.

Robert: a reduction of white wine and shallots with demi-glace and mustard.

Suprême: a poultry velouté with added cream.

Tartare: mayonnaise garnished with dill pickles, chives, and capers.

Verte: mayonnaise with spinach leaves, parsley, and lemon juice.

White Wine: a fish velouté with a white wine reduction.

Vinaigrette: oil and vinegar with chopped onions, gherkins, and herbs.

Zingara: a tomato demi-glace with shredded mush-rooms, truffles, and ham julienne.

Dish Description

Service personnel should be able to describe to guests the composition of all dishes featured on the menu and recommend items for the meal's different courses. A selection of classic and common menu items follows.

Hors d'Oeuvre

Hors d'Oeuvres are foods served before the meal or when a meal will not be served. They are bite-sized appetizers. Some examples:

COLD HORS D'OEUVRE:

Canapés: bite-sized finger foods consisting of a base of bread, toast, pastry, or cracker; a spread of butter, cheese, or pâté; and an optional topping such as caviar, smoked salmon, prawn, asparagus tip, or anchovy.

Caviar: served with buttered toast points.

Crudités: raw vegetables served with a dip.

Eggs: deviled.

Foie Gras: in terrine, in aspic, in mousse.

Lobster: lobster medallions, lobster salad.

Oysters: raw with lemon, in a cocktail.

Pâté: in terrine, in aspic, en croute.

Salami Horns: hard salami stuffed with cream cheese.

Shrimp: with cocktail sauce, stuffed, in mousse.

Salmon: smoked or gravad lox style (cured).

HOT HORS D'OEUVRE:

Barquettes: boat-shaped tartlets filled with melted cheese, foie gras, smoked salmon.

Bouchées: bite-sized pastry shells filled with cooked shrimp, creamed chicken, seafood.

Croquettes: deep-fried minced chicken, ham, or fish bound with a béchamel mixture.

Mushrooms: stuffed with crab meat.

Oysters: Mornay (broiled with Mornay sauce), casino (broiled with bacon).

Quiche: (miniature) Lorraine, with bacon and onions; Florentine, with spinach.

Rumaki: chicken livers and water chestnuts wrapped in bacon.

Appetizers

Appetizers, traditionally, are the first course or introduction to the meal. The nature of the appetizer generally depends on the composition of the main dish; that is, if the main dish is heavy, the appetizer should be light and vice versa. The following are examples of appetizers.

Antipasto: a selection of cold foods, such as hard salami, olives, marinated artichoke, Parma ham, and cheese.

Artichoke Vinaigrette: steamed artichoke served with vinaigrette sauce.

Asparagus Hollandaise: steamed asparagus and hollandaise sauce.

Fruit Cup: a selection of fresh fruit bits.

Prosciutto and Melon: thin-sliced Parma ham served with slices of ripe melon.

Salmon Gratin: poached salmon fillet with cream sauce, browned.

Seafood Cocktail: shellfish served with cocktail sauce.

Vegetables Tempura: vegetable pieces coated in tempura batter and deep-fried.

Salads

Salads are versatile dishes that can be served as a first course, before the main dish, as a main dish, with the main dish, or after it. Presented below are some typical salads seen on menus.

Caesar: romaine lettuce with croutons and Parmesan cheese, dressed with anchovies, garlic, and chopped coddled egg.

Chef's: green salad with sliced turkey, ham, cheese, quartered hard-boiled eggs, and tomato wedges.

Elizabeth: Boston lettuce with lemon juice and fresh cream.

Green: mixed salad greens torn in bite-size pieces.

Niçoise: diced cooked potatoes and green beans with vinaigrette sauce, garnished with anchovies, black olives, and tomato wedges.

Rachel: celery, artichoke hearts, and cooked potatoes with mayonnaise, garnished with asparagus tips.

Vegetables à la Grecque: boiled vegetables marinated in olive oil and herbs.

Waldorf: celery, apples, and mayonnaise garnished with walnuts.

Salad Dressings

Most salad dressings have either a vinegar-oil base or an egg-oil emulsion base. Here are some examples:

VINEGAR-OIL:

Italian: oil, vinegar, garlic, and oregano.

Vinaigrette: oil, vinegar, and seasonings.

EGG-OIL EMULSION:

Blue Cheese: mayonnaise, blue cheese, and seasonings.

French: oil, vinegar, eggs, and seasonings.

Green Goddess: mayonnaise, sour cream, anchovies, parsley, and seasonings.

Ranch: mayonnaise, buttermilk, parsley, garlic, and onion.

Russian: mayonnaise, pickle relish, hard-boiled egg, and pimiento.

Thousand Island: mayonnaise, chili sauce, hard-boiled egg, and chopped dill pickles.

Soups

Soups may be served at the beginning of the meal, after the appetizer, or as a main dish. They fall into two major categories, clear and thick, according to the method of preparation and the ingredients.

CLEAR SOUPS: Clear soups are unthickened, translucent liquids made with stock. The simplest clear soup is the **broth,** which is just a seasoned stock. Other common clear soups are:

French Onion: a clear soup garnished with a slice of toasted bread spread with a butter-and-cheese paste.

Vegetable: a soup of stock, diced vegetables, and flavor-building herbs.

Minestrone: a vegetable soup with white beans, pasta, and Parmesan cheese.

Avgolemono: a Greek soup made with chicken stock, egg, and lemon juice.

Consommés are strong, clear broths or stocks that have been clarified. They can be made from poultry, beef, fish, or vegetable stock. These classic soups often take the name of the garnishes put in them before serving. Some of the more well-known are:

Brunoise: garnished with finely diced vegetables.

Carmen: with rice, shredded peppers, and diced tomatoes.

Caroline: garnished with cooked rice.

Célestine: garnished with shredded mixed-herb crêpes.

Chasseur: garnished with shredded mushrooms and croutons.

Double: concentrated consommé.

Julienne: garnished with assorted shredded vegetables.

Madrilène: chicken consommé with diced tomatoes, Madeira wine, and brandy.

Nelson: fish stock garnished with rice and cubed lobster.

Olga: garnished with shredded vegetables and port wine.

Parisian: garnished with leeks and potatoes.

Printanière: garnished with sliced vegetables.

Reine: garnished with tapioca and shredded poultry meat.

Royal: garnished with cubed custard.

Vermicelli: garnished with broken, very thin spaghetti.

Xavier: garnished with egg drops and parsley.

Thick Soups: Thick soups can be divided into **creams** and **purees,** and **bisques, chowders,** and **gumbos.**

Like consommés, they are named after their main ingredients and garnishes.

Cream soups may be thickened with milk, cream, and roux. Some famous cream soups:

American: a tomato cream soup garnished with shrimp and rice.

Argenteuil: an asparagus cream soup.

Cardinal: a fish cream soup flavored with lobster stock.

Carmen: a tomato cream soup garnished with diced tomatoes.

Caroline: a rice cream soup.

Diane: a game cream soup with port wine.

Dubarry: a cauliflower cream soup.

Princess: a poultry cream soup garnished with asparagus tips.

Reine: a poultry cream soup with rice.

Washington: a cream of corn soup.

Purée soups are thickened with puréed, starchy vegetables. Sometimes they are finished with cream or milk, in which case they are very similar to cream soups. The following are classic purée soups:

Ambassadeur: a green pea purée garnished with sorrel, lettuce, and rice.

Bonne Femme: an onion, leek, and potato soup.

Clamart: a purée of fresh green peas garnished with croutons.

Condé: a purée of red beans.

Crécy: a purée of carrots and potatoes.

Esau: a lentil purée.

Garbure: a purée of vegetables.

Jackson: a purée of potatoes garnished with tapioca and shredded leeks.

Lamballe: a purée of fresh peas and tapioca.

Parisian: a leek and potato soup garnished with croutons.

Parmentier: a purée of potatoes.

Saint Germain: a purée of green peas garnished with croutons.

Bisques are thick soups with a shrimp, lobster, or crayfish base. They are thickened with rice or roux and have added to them puréed shellfish. Chowders are hearty soups made with fish, shellfish, or vegetables, and generally have potatoes and salt pork or bacon added for flavor. Gumbos are made with meat and/or fish and vegetables, and are often flavored with hot peppers, okra, and ground sassafras. Some examples of these three types of soup are:

Shrimp Bisque: made with puréed shrimp, cream, and roux, and flavored with sherry or brandy.

New England Clam Chowder: made with milk.

Manhattan Clam Chowder: made with tomatoes.

Louisiana Chicken Gumbo: made with chicken stock, okra, filé, and seasonings.

Some consommés and cream soups are often served cold in warm weather. Other cold soups are made with puréed fruits or diced salad vegetables. Examples are:

Fruited Yogurt Soups: made with puréed fruits, orange juice, and plain yogurt.

Gazpacho: made with diced salad vegetables and bread crumbs, and flavored with garlic, olive oil, and vinegar.

Vichyssoise: a chicken stock with puréed leeks and potatoes, butter, and heavy cream.

Eggs and Omelets

Eggs are always featured on breakfast menus, and sometimes they are presented between the first and the main courses on lunch or dinner menus. The most common methods of serving eggs are:

BAKED OR SHIRRED: Eggs prepared this way are cooked in the oven or bain-marie in a baking dish with butter.

Florentine: on a bed of spinach.

Portuguese: with crushed tomatoes.

Reine: with diced, creamed poultry meat.

Zingara: with zingara sauce.

POACHED: Fresh whole eggs are simmered in water and served in the following ways:

Argenteuil: with asparagus tips and cream sauce.

Benedict: on toast or an English muffin, with ham or Canadian bacon and hollandaise sauce.

Bombay: on a bed of rice pilaf with curry sauce.

Chasseur: with chicken livers and mushrooms.

Duchess: on duchess potatoes.

English Style: on buttered toast.

Florentine: on spinach with Mornay sauce.

Montglas: with diced ham, foie gras, truffles, and Madeira sauce.

Nantua: with diced shrimp or lobster and Nantua sauce.

Rossini: with foie gras and Madeira sauce.

FRIED: Eggs can be cooked to different levels of done-ness: "sunny-side up"—a runny, soft yolk; "over easy"—flipped over, the yolk still runny; "medium"—flipped over, the yolk slightly thickened; and "hard"—flipped over, the yolk fully set. Some ways of serving fried eggs are:

American Style: with grilled tomatoes and bacon.

Colbert: with small grilled sausages.

Forestière: with morel mushrooms.

Lorraine: with slices of Gruyère cheese and bacon.

Opéra: with chicken livers, asparagus tips, and Madeira sauce.

Portuguese: with crushed tomatoes.

Victoria: with chopped lobster or crayfish.

Yorkshire: with sliced ham and tomato sauce.

SCRAMBLED: Some ways to present scrambled eggs are:

Forestière: with mushrooms.

Parmentier: with sautéed diced potatoes.

Spanish Style: with fried diced tomatoes and pimientos.

Yvette: with asparagus tips and chopped shrimp.

OMELETS: Omelets can be rolled, or French style, or flat, also known as farmer style or *frittata*. They can be pre-pared with different garnishes, such as:

Chasseur: with chicken livers and mushrooms.

Lorraine: with bacon and cheese.

Lyonnaise: with onions.

Niçoise: with crushed tomatoes and diced artichoke hearts.

Parmentier: with potatoes.

Paysanne: with potatoes, onions, and bacon.

Savoyarde: with potatoes and cheese.

Spanish: with tomatoes, peppers, and onions.

Western: with onions, green peppers, and chopped ham.

Seafood

Common cuts of fish are:

Fillet: boneless side of fish
Steak: crosscut of fish body
Stick: crosscut of fillet
Paupiette: rolled fillet
Darne: thick fish steak

Fin fish and shellfish can be prepared in different ways. The most common methods follow.

Deep-Fried: coated in milk and flour or batter, and cooked in very hot deep oil. Fried fish should be transported uncovered from the kitchen to the table. Cold sauces, such as tartare or rémoulade, may be offered with it.

en Papillote: the seafood and flavorings are wrapped in parchment paper and cooked in a hot oven.

Grilled: can be accompanied by a compound butter, such as maître d'hôtel.

Matelote: poached in a red wine fumet.

Meunière: pan-fried in butter with lemon juice and chopped parsley.

Poached: cooked in an acidic, aromatic stock or fumet.

Sautéed: pan-fried in a small amount of fat.

Seafood can be served with different garnishes, which give the dishes names such as:

Amandine: sautéed, garnished with sliced almonds, parsley, and lemon juice.

Ambassador: poached, served on a mushroom purée with white wine sauce.

Bagration: poached, with Mornay sauce and shredded truffles.

Bordelaise: poached, served with red wine sauce and mushrooms.

Cardinal: poached, with cardinal sauce, lobster medallions, and truffles.

Colbert: fried, served with maître d'hôtel butter.

Dieppoise: poached, finished with white wine sauce, mussels, and shrimps.

Doria: meunière, garnished with cucumbers.

Dugleré: poached, served in white wine sauce with crushed tomatoes.

Florentine: poached, served on a bed of spinach with Mornay sauce.

Grenobloise: meunière, with capers, lemon, and anchovies.

Maître d'Hôtel: grilled, served with maître d'hôtel butter.

Marinière: poached, finished with white wine sauce, mussels, and shallots.

Mornay: poached, served with Mornay sauce.

Normande: poached, served with white wine sauce, oysters, mussels, and shrimp.

Opéra: poached, served with white wine sauce, asparagus tips, and truffles.

Riviera: meunière, with mushrooms and chopped artichoke hearts.

Véronique: poached, finished with creamed hollandaise sauce and seedless green grapes.

Walewska: poached, served with lobster medallions, mushrooms, and Mornay sauce.

Pasta, Dumplings, and Rice

Pasta dishes can be served as appetizers, first courses, and entrées. Common pasta shapes are spaghetti, linguine, fettucine, macaroni, and noodles. Some pasta dishes are:

Alfredo: with butter, heavy cream, and Parmesan cheese.

Bolognaise: with meat sauce.

Carbonara: with ham julienne and mushrooms in cream sauce.

Gratin: with butter mixed with a thin cream sauce, covered with grated cheese and gratinated.

Marinara: in a spicy tomato sauce.

Milanaise: au gratin, garnished with shredded ham and mushrooms, bound in a demi-glace.

Napolitaine: with tomato sauce.

Pesto: with fresh basil sauce made with olive oil.

Puttanesca: with olive oil, tomatoes, black olives, capers, anchovies, and herbs.

Tetrazzine: with shredded poultry meat, mushrooms, and cream.

GNOCCHI: Gnocchi are small dumplings made with semolina flour, puréed potatoes, or puff pastry dough. They are featured on menus as:

Parisian: made with cream puff pastry dough.

Piémontaise: made with mashed potatoes and flour dough.

Romaine: made with semolina flour, milk, eggs, and cheese.

Spatzli: narrow strips of flour, egg, and milk batter sautéed in butter.

RICE: Rice often substitutes for potatoes as the starch of entrée garnitures. Here are a few common ways of featuring rice on menus:

Créole: boiled and cooled, then reheated in a buttered pan.

Milanaise: risotto made with saffron rice.

Pilaf: boiled in stock with diced onions and butter.

Risi Bisi: risotto with cooked peas and parsley.

Risotto: pilaf bound with butter and Parmesan cheese.

Meat and Poultry

BEEF: Beef is meat from cattle butchered from the age of 15 weeks. Beef products are considered to be red meat. The main wholesale beef cuts are:

Brisket: the breast muscle.

Chuck: cut between the neck and the shoulder blade.

Flank: the underbelly muscle.

Loin: the back muscle between the false ribs and the hipbone.

Rib: cut between the shoulder blade and the loin.

Round: the leg muscle.

Tenderloin: the boneless loin.

Once portioned, fabricated cuts take names such as:

Chateaubriand: a thick center cut of tenderloin.

Club: steak from the loin.

Delmonico: rib eye steak.

Entrecôte: rib steak.

Filet Mignon: thick tenderloin cut.

New York: loin steak.

Porterhouse: loin steak.

T-Bone: loin steak.

Tournedos: a small tenderloin steak.

Garnishes, sauces, and methods of cooking give beef names that are common on restaurant menus. For example:

Au Jus: served with its own juice.

Bouquetière: garnished with assorted vegetables.

Bourguignonne: braised and garnished with small onions, bacon, and mushrooms.

Carbonnade: beef slices braised in brown stock with onions and other vegetables.

Clamart: garnished with artichoke bottoms filled with peas.

Dubarry: garnished with sprigs of cauliflower.

Forestière: garnished with mushrooms.

Goulash: braised cubes of beef with onions, paprika, bacon, and red wine.

Helder: served with crushed tomatoes and béarnaise sauce.

Judic: garnished with braised lettuce.

London Broil: grilled marinated flank steak.

Lyonnaise: served with buttered, chopped onions.

Marchand de Vin: served with a red wine demi-glace.

Parisian: served with Parisian potatoes and braised lettuce.

Princess: garnished with a bouquet of asparagus tips.

Provençale: served with tomatoes, mushrooms, black olives, and anchovy fillets.

Rossini: served with a slice of foie gras, truffles, and Madeira sauce.

Stroganoff: diced, sautéed, and stewed in a demi-glace thickened with sour cream.

Wellington: roasted, covered with forcemeat, and baked in a puff pastry crust.

VEAL: Veal comes from cattle younger than 15 weeks and is considered white meat. The prime cuts are similar to those for beef. The following names are generally given to veal cuts:

Grenadin: a thick slice cut from the round of the leg.

Osso Buco: a shank cross slice that includes the bone.

Scaloppine: a thin slice cut from the leg.

Here are some common ways of featuring veal on restaurant menus:

Blanquette: stewed veal cubes in a rich velouté sauce.

Bonne Femme: fried, with bacon pieces and small onions.

Cordon Bleu: ham and cheese sandwiched in two breaded veal scaloppine, which are then fried.

Fermière: in a casserole with assorted vegetables.

Milanaise: dipped and fried, garnished with spaghetti Milanaise.

Pojarski: ground and mixed with sautéed onions and cream, then chopped, shaped, breaded, and fried.

Saltimbocca: scaloppine and prosciutto ham, dredged in flour and sautéed; served with a white or Marsala wine sauce.

Wienerschnitzel: dipped, fried, and garnished with anchovy fillets and capers.

Zingara: fried, with shredded tongue, ham, mushrooms, and zingara sauce.

LAMB: Cuts of lamb are considered red meat. Two common ways of featuring lamb on menus are as cutlets and chops in the following dishes:

Boulangère: garnished with boulangère potatoes.

Bretonne: fried, served with navy or lima beans.

Champvalon: fried with onions, garlic, and parsley.

Montmorency: fried, garnished with artichoke hearts and asparagus tips.

Parisian: grilled, with asparagus tips and Parisian potatoes.

Provençale: fried, served with crushed tomatoes, garlic, and black olives.

Lamb leg and shoulder are also served, in the following ways:

Boulangère: roast, garnished with boulangère potatoes.

Fricassée: seared lamb cubes stewed in a pale roux.

Irish Stew: stewed lamb cubes with onions, leeks, celery, and potatoes.

Navarin: stewed in a brown sauce with carrots, onions, and peas.

Nivernaise: roasted with carrots and small onions.

Shish Kebab: marinated lamb cubes and vegetables broiled on a skewer.

Vert-Pré: grilled, garnished with green beans or watercress.

PORK: Pork is considered white meat. Common ways of preparing pork are:

Bourguignonne: braised in red wine with mushrooms and small onions.

Charcutière: fried, with Robert sauce and julienne of pickles.

Flamande: fried with sliced sautéed apples.

Milanaise: fried, garnished with spaghetti Milanaise.

Normande: fried, served with apple sauce.

Robert: grilled, served with Robert sauce.

POULTRY: The term *poultry* applies to edible birds domestically raised. A spring chicken is two to three months old; a capon is a fat, castrated male; and a rock cornish hen is a baby female five to seven weeks old. Poultry is often served in the following ways:

À la King: diced, in cream sauce with mushrooms and pimientos.

Ancienne: fried, with small onions, mushrooms, and croutons.

Bonne Femme: roasted, with potatoes, bacon pieces, and small onions.

Cacciatora: breaded, sautéed, and then baked in tomato sauce.

Chasseur: fried with mushrooms.

Coq au Vin: braised with red wine.

Demidoff: fried with turnips, carrots, and truffles.

Deviled: coated with spicy bread crumbs and broiled.

Florentine: poached, served on creamed spinach.

Fricassée: braised in a blond sauce.

Kiev: a rolled, breaded chicken breast filled with butter and deep-fried.

Marengo: sautéed, then braised in a brown sauce with onions and mushrooms.

Maryland: breaded, deep-fried, and served in a cream sauce, garnished with grilled bacon and corn fritters.

Princesse: poached, with a suprême sauce and asparagus tips.

Tetrazzini: boiled chicken strips in cream sauce, served on pasta.

DUCK AND GOOSE:

À l'Orange: braised with a demi-glace made with orange juice and shredded peel.

Bigarade: braised, with bigarade sauce.

Nivernaise: roasted, garnished with pearl onions and carrots.

With Olives: braised, garnished with green olives.

PHEASANT, PARTRIDGE, AND QUAIL:

Périgourdine: served in a casserole with truffles and mushrooms.

Salmis: roasted, then cooked in a game demi-glace with wine.

Smitane: sautéed, covered with reduced onions, sour cream, and tomato demi-glace.

Souvaroff: stuffed with foie gras and truffles, and baked in a casserole sealed with pastry dough.

FURRED GAME: Furred game includes venison and hare and rabbit, served in the following ways:

Baden-Baden: sautéed venison with a demi-glace with white wine and cream.

Cumberland: roast saddle of venison with chestnut purée and Cumberland sauce.

Grand Veneur: roast saddle of venison with chestnut purée and grand veneur sauce.

Hunter Style: sautéed venison garnished with mushrooms.

Nesselrode: fried venison garnished with chestnut purée and poivrade sauce.

Civet: marinated hare or rabbit stewed in red wine with the blood of the animal.

Forestière: roasted hare or rabbit garnished with mushrooms, glazed chestnuts, and poivrade sauce.

Saint Hubert: roasted hare or rabbit served in a poivrade sauce.

Vegetables

POTATOES: Besides the well-known styles (shoestring, french-fried, steak cut, and straw), potatoes appear on menus under many different names. These are most common:

Anna: sliced, layered in a mold with butter, and baked.

Berny: croquette potatoes with minced truffles, dusted with ground almonds and fried.

Boulangère: sliced, with onions and stock, and baked.

Château: oval-shaped, blanched and roasted.

Croquette: puréed, combined with egg yolk, shaped as cylinders, and dipped and fried.

Dauphine: puréed, mixed with choux paste, formed into elongated shapes, and fried.

Duchess: mashed with butter and egg yolks, piped into small mounds, and baked.

Gaufrettes: cut in a waffle pattern and deep-fried.

Gratin: puréed, covered with grated cheese, and browned in the oven.

Lorette: same as for dauphine, but mixed with grated cheese.

Lyonnaise: sliced and sautéed with onions.

Maître d'Hôtel: cooked in cream and sprinkled with parsley.

Mousseline: puréed with whipped cream.

Noisette: cut to the size of hazelnuts, blanched, brushed with butter, and browned.

O'Brien: sautéed, diced, and garnished with bacon, onions, and green peppers.

Parisienne: same as for noisette but slightly larger.

Parmentier: roast, cut in large cubes.

Paysanne: cooked in stock, with bacon.

Pont-Neuf: fried, cut in large square sticks.

Rissolées: quite brown chateau potatoes.

Savoyarde: sliced, baked with grated cheese and chicken stock.

Voisin: same as for Anna potatoes, but with grated Swiss cheese.

ARTICHOKES:

Argenteuil: hearts, filled with asparagus tips.

Clamart: hearts, with green peas and carrots.

Florentine: hearts, with spinach leaves, Mornay sauce, gratinated.

Hollandaise: boiled, served with separate hollandaise sauce.

Vinaigrette: boiled, served cold with separate vinaigrette.

ASPARAGUS:

Cold: boiled, served with mayonnaise or vinaigrette.

Mornay: boiled, nappé with Mornay sauce and gratinated.

Milanaise: boiled, sprinkled with cheese and melted butter, and gratinated.

CARROTS:

Glazed: boiled, sautéed with a touch of sugar.

Purée: boiled, crushed, buttered, and creamed.

Vichy: sliced, boiled, and glazed in butter.

CAULIFLOWER:

Anglaise: boiled, covered with melted butter and parsley.

Italian: boiled, buttered, and nappé with tomato sauce.

Polonaise: boiled, covered with chopped hard-boiled egg, bread crumbs, and browned butter.

GREEN BEANS:

Amandine: sautéed with sliced almonds.

Maître d'Hôtel: boiled, bound with a light béchamel sauce.

Portugaise: boiled, then sautéed with crushed tomatoes.

MUSHROOMS:

Bordelaise: sautéed with shallots and chopped parsley.

Creamed: stewed in butter and bound with cream.

Provençale: sautéed in olive oil with onions, garlic, and herbs.

PEAS:

Bonne Femme: cooked with small onions and shredded lettuce, and garnished with pieces of bacon.

Flamande: boiled, with small carrots.

Française: same as for bonne femme, but without bacon.

TOMATOES:

Concassées: diced, stewed in butter with onions.

Italian: halved, stuffed with risotto.

Provençale: halved, covered with bread crumbs, garlic, and parsley.

Ratatouille: tomatoes, onions, peppers, eggplant, zucchini and herbs, sautéed in olive oil.

Desserts

BAVARIANS: A bavarian is a custard sauce with gelatin and whipped cream. Common flavors are chocolate, coffee, and kirsch. Other Bavarians are:

Charlotte Royale: on a jelly roll base, flavored with kirsch.

Charlotte Russe: on a ladyfinger base, flavored with kirsch.

Diplomat: combined with sponge cake drizzled with rum.

CAKES: Some specialty cakes commonly offered in restaurants follow.

Black Forest: chocolate sponge cake with red cherries between the layers, flavored with kirsch.

Kugelhupf: diced candied fruits folded in cake batter and baked in a special kugelhupf mold.

Napoleons (Millefeuilles): cream filling between layers of puff pastry; frosted with fondant icing.

COUPES (SUNDAES): A coupe consists of ice cream and fruit served in a shallow, stemmed glass. Famous coupes offered on dining room menus are:

Alexandra: fruit salad with kirsch and strawberry ice cream.

Hélène: half a canned pear with vanilla ice cream and hot chocolate sauce.

Jacques: fruit salad with lemon sherbet and strawberry ice cream.

Jamaica: diced pineapple with rum and coffee ice cream.

Melba: half a canned peach, vanilla ice cream, and melba sauce.

Montmorency: cherries with kirsch and vanilla ice cream.

Romanoff: fresh strawberries with kirsch and vanilla ice cream.

Royale: fruit salad with kirsch and vanilla ice cream.

FLAMED DESSERTS: These elegant desserts are generally prepared or served tableside:

Baked Alaska: ice cream over a sponge cake base, covered with meringue and glazed in a very hot oven for a short period. Flamed with brandy.

Cherries Jubilée: hot bing cherries over vanilla ice cream, flamed with kirsch.

Crêpes Suzette: thin pancakes with orange and lemon juice and Grand Marnier liqueur. Flamed with brandy.

PUDDINGS: Puddings are a mixture of milk, sugar, butter, and eggs, thickened with cornstarch. Baked puddings contain additional ingredients such as rice or bread.

Blancmange English Style: made with vanilla or almond extract.

Blancmange French Style: made with almond milk and gelatin.

Crème Anglaise (Custard): lightly thickened, flavored with vanilla.

Cabinet: a base of sponge cake and raisins.

Montmorency: with cherries.

SOUFFLÉS: A soufflé is a mixture of flour, sugar, milk, butter, and eggs cooked slowly in the oven. Common flavors are almond, chocolate, lemon, strawberry, and liqueurs. A popular soufflé is the **Rothschild,** which is lemon-flavored, with pitted cherries and strawberries.

TORTES: A torte can be made with fruits and nuts. Three specialty tortes are:

Dobos: cake layers sandwiched with mocha buttercream.

Linzer: flour dough with hazelnuts and rum, filled with raspberry jam and covered with latticed dough strips.

Sacher: apricot preserves between chocolate cake layers, covered with chocolate glaze.

OTHER DESSERTS:

Apple Strudel: baked phyllo pastry filled with sautéed diced apples, raisins, and cinnamon.

Pétits Fours: bite-sized glazed cakes made of génoise.

Pithiviers: baked puff pastry circles filled with pastry cream and frangipane.

Sabayon: egg yolks, sugar, and dessert wine (usually Marsala), thickened over gentle heat and served hot.

Culinary Terms

Listed below are culinary terms often found on restaurant menus. Serving personnel should be able to recognize these and explain them to guests.

Al dente: firm to the bite.

Aspic: a jelly of stock and gelatin.

Brioche: a rich dough made with eggs and butter.

Cassoulet: a stew made with dry beans and meat.

Chafing Dish: a heated metal dish in which foods are kept warm in buffet service.

Chef de Rang: front waiter.

Choucroute: sauerkraut.

Cioppino: fish stew.

Compote: stewed fruit.

Concassé: chopped.

Confit: meat that has been cooked and preserved in its own fat.

Cornichon: a small, sour pickle.

Coulibiac: fish baked in a pastry crust with rice, onions, and mushrooms.

Coulis: a thick purée.

Couscous: semolina starch.

Crème Brulée: custard topped with caramelized sugar.

Crème Fraîche: whipping cream.

en Croute: encased in pastry crust.

Curry: a mixture of Indian spices.

Daube: a meat stew braised in red wine.

Emincé: cut into very thin slices.

Escalope: a small, flat piece of meat.

Estouffade: stew.

Farce: stuffing.

Farci: stuffed.

Farina: wheat flour.

Filé: a spice made from dried sassafras root.

Fond: stock.

Fondant: icing used in pastry making.

Forcemeat: a mixture of ground meat and flavorings.

Galantine: boned meat, stuffed, poached, and pressed; served cold.

Garni: garnished.

Génoise: a sponge cake.

Gherkin: a small pickle.

Glace: glazed.

Granité: water ice.

Kasha: buckwheat groats.

Kirsch: cherry brandy.

Kosher: prepared according to Jewish dietary specifications.

Lox: cured salmon.

Maître d'Hôtel: head waiter.

Marbling: specks of fat found in beef.

Marzipan: ground almonds with sugar and egg whites.

Matignon: edible mirepoix.

Méringue: sweetened, beaten egg whites.

Mise en Place: preparation for service.

Nappé: coated with sauce.

Paella: a Spanish rice dish with meat and shellfish, seasoned with saffron.

Paillarde: a thin scallop of meat.

Paupiette: a thin cut of meat or fish rolled, stuffed, and poached or braised.

Phyllo Dough: a type of puff pastry dough.

Quenelle: a light, poached dumpling.

Ragout: stew.

Ramekin: a small, ceramic dish.

Rôti: roasted.

Roulade: a slice of meat stuffed and rolled.

Sommelier: wine steward.

Sous-Chef: under-chef.

Sweetbreads: the thymus gland of calves.

Tart: a pie without a top crust.

Tartlet: a small, individual tart.

Tempura: food battered and deep-fried.

Timbale: food served pail-shaped.

Wok: a round-bottomed pan made of rolled steel.

PART FOUR

Bar Service

The success of a bar operation depends on the disposition and trade savvy of its service personnel. Bar staff should be friendly, attentive, and honest, as well as good entertainers. At the same time, they must have a thorough knowledge of drinks and be able to identify guests' requests and explain the components of drinks.

Serving Alcoholic Drinks

Beverages should be served on a tray, from the right of the guest. Glasses, with the exception of wine and champagne glasses, must be placed on a saucer, doily, or cocktail napkin. Premium brands should be poured in front of the guest.

Serving staff should recognize habitual customers and remember what they regularly order to drink. Anticipating a guest's order endears the establishment to the guest. Both servers and bartenders must know the recipes of popular and traditional mixed drinks and be able to work very quickly under pressure.

Serving Alcohol and the Law

The Dram Shop acts establish civil liabilities on servers if an intoxicated patron causes harm to a third party. Service personnel must be aware of the implications of these acts: The establishment—not the intoxicated guest or injured third party—has the burden of responsibility. It is therefore important that employees serving alcoholic beverages refuse to serve guests who appear intoxicated. An elegant way of "cutting off" a customer is to offer him or her a cup of coffee or an alcohol-free beverage on the house.

The law again sets the burden of responsibility on the establishment if alcoholic drinks are served to minors. If there is any doubt about a guest's age, servers should ask for proof of date of birth.

Bar Glassware

There are three major types of glassware: tumbler, or flat-bottomed glass without a foot; footed, if the bowl sits on a base; and stem, if the bowl is separated from the base. Most glasses are named for the drinks usually served in them (Fig. 40). Common sizes found in beverage operations include:

> *Highball:* 8-ounce;
> *Rocks:* 5-ounce;
> *Collins:* 12-ounce;
> *Sherry:* 2-ounce;
> *Snifter:* 10-ounce;
> *Wine:* 8-ounce.

Types of Alcoholic Beverages

The alcohol content of fermented beverages (wine and beer) is measured by volume: Table wines range between

Fig. 40. Common bar glassware.

7 and 14 percent; beer, between 3 and 10 percent. The alcohol content in distilled spirits is expressed as *proof,* which is twice the alcohol by volume. Thus, an 80-proof spirit has an alcohol content by volume of 40 percent.

Besides wines, the beverages served in bars can be divided into the following categories: beers, aperitifs, dessert wines, spirits, liqueurs, alcohol-free drinks, and mixed drinks. Bar service personnel must have a thorough knowledge of all of them.

BEER

Beer is made from germinated barley that is roasted to a pale or dark degree to produce light or brown varieties. The mashed liquid is brewed (boiled) for several hours and flavored with hops. It is then fermented by yeast and matured in storage.

Ale: a malt beverage, darker, heavier, and more bitter than beer, containing about 6 percent alcohol by volume.

Bock: a dark beer with a rich, sweet taste.

Malt Liquor: a malt beverage with a higher alcohol content than beer and a stronger, hoppier taste.

Stout: a very dark and quite bitter beer.

All beers should be served in grease-free glasses, since a trace of grease will destroy the froth and make the beer look flat. For this reason, beer glasses should be washed and dried very carefully. Bottled beer should be poured down the center of the glass when served to the guest. Draught beer should be poured with the glass held at a 45-degree angle until it is about half full; the glass is then straightened, with the rest of the beer poured down the center. A collar of froth one-half to one inch thick should top the glass.

APERITIFS

Appetizer drinks are very common in Europe, where people consume them before meals instead of cocktails. The most common aperitifs are the following:

Anises: drinks with a base of aniseed liqueur and an alcohol content of about 45 percent. They are always served with iced water, which makes the drink look milky. Famous French brands are Pernod, Ricard, and Berger.

Bitters: like vermouth, wine-based products in which plant roots and barks, such as quinine, are added. France produces Dubonnet, Amer Picon, Byrrh, and Saint Raphael. Cynar, Campari, and Fernet Branca are products of Italy.

Vermouths: fortified sweet or dry wines to which aromatic herbs are added. Their alcohol content is 16 to 18 percent. Famous international brands of vermouth are Martini and Cinzano from Italy and Noilly-Prat and Richard from France.

DESSERT WINES

Dessert wines are fortified, sweet wines that come mainly from California and southern Europe. Their alcohol content varies from 15 to 22 percent, and they are generally drunk after meals, although sometimes they can be requested as aperitifs. In cooking, these wines are the base for major sauces.

Madeira: produced on the Portuguese island of Madeira in the North Atlantic. When aged, it is clear-white, sweet, and aromatic.

Marsala: comes from the island of Sicily. It is aged in barrels exposed to the sun, which gives the wine a special, sweet bouquet.

Port: named for the region of Oporto in Northern Portugal. It is quite sweet and a favorite in Great Britain, where it has been imported since the sixteenth century.

Sherry: comes from the region of Jerez de la Frontera in southern Spain. It is fortified with brandy and matured in oak barrels for up to 20 years. As with port, England has been the major consumer of sherry for generations. Sherries can be dry or very dry, in which case they are a perfect complement to appetizers. Sweet or cream sherries can be served as aperitifs, with desserts, or after a meal.

Spirits

Spirits are obtained by distilling a fermented liquid of vegetable origin. The alcohol content of spirits is very high, ranging from 80 to 155 proof.

Armagnac: a French brandy produced in the Armagnac region. It is dry and full-bodied.

Brandy: distilled from grape wines or from the fermented juice of fruits. When made from grapes, it is a smooth spirit of great bouquet similar to cognac. Brandy should be served in a snifter.

Cognac: a brandy distilled in the Charente region of France. Only brandies made in this area may be denominated *cognac*. This spirit gets its distinctive taste and color from the oak wood in which it is aged. The quality of cognac is identified by stars in ascending order of quality and by letters. For instance:

***—good quality, aged at least five years
V.O.—very old
V.O.P.—very old pale
V.O.S.P.—very old soft pale

Famous cognacs are Courvoisier, Hennessey, Martell, and Remy Martin.

Gin: the product of grain spirits flavored with juniper berries and spices. When served straight, it should be very cold.

Rum: made by distilling fermented sugar cane or sugar molasses. The main rum-producing areas are the Caribbean islands of Puerto Rico, Jamaica, and Barbados.

Tequila: distilled from the fermented sap of the agave plant. When aged in oak barrels, it acquires a distinct gold color. Connoisseurs drink tequila straight, with salt and lime.

Vodka: a colorless, tasteless spirit made from grain or potatoes. When ordered straight, it should be served very cold.

Whiskey: obtained by distilling malted cereals, mainly barley, corn, and rye. After distillation, whiskey is stored in oak barrels until it mellows. *Bourbon* is made mainly from fermented corn mash and aged in charred oak barrels, which provide its special flavor. *Rye* is produced from at least 51-percent rye mash and, like bourbon, is also aged in charred oak barrels. *Scotch* is produced in Scotland, mainly from sprouted barley flavored by peat smoke, which gives it a smoky taste. *Tennessee* is similar to bourbon except that after distillation it is filtered through maple charcoal, which gives it its distinct flavor.

The list of other spirits is endless, as each country distills its own specialties. Some of the best known are:

Acquavit: a dry spirit flavored with caraway. It is the national liquor of Scandinavian countries and should be served ice-cold.

Arrack: a spirit of the Far East distilled from the fermented sap of palm trees or from rice or molasses.

Calvados: a brandy produced in the Calvados region of France from fermented apple juice.

Kirsch: a colorless brandy distilled from fermented cherry juice.

Ouzo: a sweet, anise-flavored brandy from Greece.

Pisco: a strong, flavored brandy from Peru and northern Chile.

Slivovitz: a plum brandy from Yugoslavia.

LIQUEURS

Liqueurs, or cordials, are usually strong, sweet liquors, highly flavored with fruits, peels, seeds, herbs, or syrups. Cordials labeled fruit crèmes and fruit brandies are numerous. Other well-known liqueurs include:

Amaretto: almond-flavored.

Anisette: sweet, delicate, aniseed-based.

Benedictine: a secret combination of herbs originally made by Benedictine monks in France.

B & B: a Benedictine–brandy blend.

Chartreuse: aromatic, originally made by Carthusian monks.

Cointreau: orange-flavored.

Curaçao: orange-flavored, made with orange peel.

Drambuie: Scotch whiskey flavored with heather honey.

Galliano: flavored with anise and vanilla.

Grand Marnier: orange-flavored cognac.

Irish Mist: a blend of Irish whiskey and heather honey.

Kahlua: Mexican, coffee-flavored.

Maraschino: cherry- and almond-flavored.

Midori: flavored with honeydew melon.

Sloe Gin: made with blackthorn berries.

Strega: Italian, herb-flavored.

Tia Maria: Jamaican, coffee-flavored.

Triple Sec: dry, orange-flavored.

Tuaca: eggnog-cocoa brandy.

ALCOHOL-FREE DRINKS

Demand for nonalcoholic drinks is on the increase as people become more health-conscious. Fruit juices, fruit-juice-based syrups, fruit-flavored syrups, and mineral water are the standards. Other nonalcoholic drinks include:

Cardinal Punch: cranberry juice, orange juice, sweet and sour mix, and ginger ale (shaken, collins glass).

Cinderella: mango juice, pineapple juice, sweet and sour mix, and grenadine (shaken, collins glass).

Jogger: lime juice, club soda, and a lime wedge (collins glass).

Kiddy Cocktail: sweet and sour mix, grenadine, and a cherry (shaken, cocktail glass).

Prairie Oyster: tomato juice, egg yolk, salt and pepper, Tabasco, and Worcestershire sauce (mixed keeping egg yolk whole, rocks glass).

Roy Rogers: grenadine, cola, and a cherry (collins glass).

San Francisco: orange juice, pineapple juice, sweet and sour mix, grapefruit juice, grenadine, and an egg white (shaken, collins glass).

Shirley Temple: grenadine, 7-Up, and a cherry (collins glass).

Temperance Cocktail: sweet and sour mix, grenadine, and an egg yolk (shaken, cocktail glass).

Virgin Mary: Bloody Mary mix, seasonings, and a celery stalk (shaken, collins glass).

MIXED DRINKS

Typically, a mixed drink has a main alcoholic base and one or more other ingredients. Measuring the correct amounts of the components is critical. Liquors are measured in terms of jiggers (1.5 ounces) or ounces; condiments are measured by dashes (10 drops each) or drops.

Drinks containing liquids only may be stirred in a mixing glass. Drinks containing fruit juice, sugar, syrup, egg, or cream must be prepared in a shaker (see page 100). If the drink incorporates solid fruit or ice, the combination must be prepared in a blender (see page 101). Most mixed drinks fall in one of the following categories:

Highballs: combinations of a spirit and a mixer—fruit juice or water—served with ice in a highball glass (see page 102).

On the Rocks: one- or two-liquor drinks served on ice in an Old-Fashioned glass (see page 103).

Shaker/Blender Drinks: combinations of liquor, fruit, juices, mixes, and/or sugar prepared in a shaker or blender.

Pousse-Café: layers of liqueurs of different densities served in a cordial or brandy glass (see page 104).

Mixing-Glass Drinks: two or more liquors combined with ice cubes and stirred. These drinks are usually served with a garnish.

Frozen Drinks: combinations of crushed ice and drink ingredients blended until the mix is slushy. They are served in a chilled stem glass.

Cocktails: short mixed drinks consisting typically of gin, whiskey, or brandy, with different admixtures such as vermouth, fruit juices, and so forth. They are usually chilled and frequently sweetened.

COMBINATION DRINKS

The number of mixed drinks offered in bars today is incalculable. Some cocktails are eternally in demand; others come and go from one generation of bargoers to the next. A selection of traditional and contemporary mixed drinks follows.

Alexander: crème de cacao, brandy, fresh cream, nutmeg (shaken, cocktail glass).

Americano: sweet vermouth, Campari, lemon twist (rocks glass).

Angel Face: Calvados, gin, apricot brandy (shaken, cocktail glass).

Bacardi: light rum, lemon juice, grenadine (shaken, cocktail glass).

Bloody Mary: vodka, tomato juice, Worcestershire sauce, lemon juice, salt, pepper, Tabasco (mixed, highball glass).

Black Russian: vodka, Kahlua (rocks glass).

Black Velvet: Guinness beer, champagne (collins glass; do not stir).

Brave Bull: tequila, Kahlua (rocks glass).

Brown Squirrel: amaretto, dark crème de cacao, fresh cream (shaken, cocktail glass).

Champagne Cocktail: champagne, sugar cube, Angostura bitters, twist (champagne glass).

Charlie Chaplin: apricot brandy, gin, lemon juice (shaken, cocktail glass).

Chi Chi: vodka, Piña Colada mix, crushed ice, cherry (blended, highball glass).

Cobra: sloe gin, orange juice (highball glass with cube ice).

Collins: spirit, fruit juice, sugar, soda water (shaken, collins glass).

Cuba Libre: rum, cola, lemon wedge (highball glass with cube ice).

Daiquiri: light rum, lemon juice (shaken, cocktail glass).

Diablo: brandy, dry vermouth, triple sec, Angostura bitters, cherry (mixed, cocktail glass).

Easy Rider: amaretto, soda, cherry (highball glass with cube ice).

Fifty-Fifty: gin, dry vermouth (mixed, cocktail glass).

Fizz: spirit, fruit juice, sugar, soda water (shaken, 8-ounce stem glass).

Flip: spirit, egg, sugar, nutmeg (shaken, 8-ounce stem glass).

Frappé: liqueur over crushed ice (cocktail glass).

French Connection: brandy, amaretto (rocks glass).

Gibson: gin, dry vermouth, cocktail onion (mixed, cocktail glass).

Gimlet: gin, lime juice, lime squeeze (shaken, cocktail glass).

Godfather: Scotch, amaretto (rocks glass).

Golden Cadillac: Galliano, light crème de cacao, fresh cream (shaken, cocktail glass).

Grasshopper: crème de menthe, crème de cacao, fresh cream (blended, cocktail glass).

Gypsy: vodka, Benedictine, Angostura bitters (shaken, cocktail glass).

Harvey Wallbanger: vodka, Galliano, orange juice (highball glass with cube ice).

Irish Coffee: Irish whiskey, coffee, sugar, whipped cream (coffee mug).

Jack Rose: apple brandy, lemon juice, grenadine (shaken, cocktail glass).

Kir: white wine, crème de cassis (8-ounce wine glass with cube ice).

Lady: Canadian whiskey, pineapple juice, anisette, Angostura bitters (shaken, cocktail glass).

Mamie Taylor: Scotch, ginger ale, lemon twist (highball glass).

Manhattan: Canadian or bourbon whiskey, sweet vermouth, Angostura bitters, stemmed cherry (mixed, cocktail glass).

Margarita: tequila, triple sec, lime juice (shaken or blended, salt-rimmed Margarita glass).

Martini: gin, dry vermouth, olives (mixed, cocktail glass).

Mist: spirit over crushed ice, lemon twist (rocks glass).

Negroni: gin, sweet vermouth, Campari, twist (mixed, cocktail glass).

Old-Fashioned: bourbon, Angostura bitters, sugar, club soda, orange slice, cherry (Old-Fashioned glass).

Orange Blossom: gin, orange juice (mixed, cocktail glass).

Perfect Manhattan: Canadian or bourbon whiskey, dry vermouth, sweet vermouth, lemon twist (mixed, cocktail glass).

Perfect Martini: gin, dry vermouth, sweet vermouth, olive (mixed, cocktail glass).

Pink Lady: gin, grenadine, fresh cream (shaken, cocktail glass).

Pink Squirrel: light crème de cacao, cream of almond, fresh cream (shaken, cocktail glass).

Rob Roy: Scotch, sweet vermouth, Angostura bitters, stemmed cherry (mixed, cocktail glass).

Rusty Nail: Scotch, Drambuie (rocks glass).

Salty Dog: vodka, grapefruit juice (salt-rimmed collins glass).

Scorpion: rum, brandy, orange juice, lemon juice, orgeat syrup (shaken, collins glass).

Screwdriver: vodka, orange juice (highball glass with cube ice).

Sidecar: brandy, Cointreau, lemon juice (shaken, sugar-rimmed cocktail glass).

Silver Bullet: gin, Scotch, lemon twist (mixed, cocktail glass).

Singapore Sling: gin, cherry brandy, lemon juice, sugar, club soda (shaken, collins glass).

Sour: spirit, lemon juice, sugar, cherry, orange slice (shaken, rocks glass).

Spritzer: white wine, soda water, lemon slice (wine or highball glass).

Stinger: brandy, white crème de menthe (rocks glass).

Susie Taylor: rum, ginger ale, half-squizzed lime in glass (collins glass).

Tango: gin, sweet vermouth, triple sec (mixed, cocktail glass).

White Russian: vodka, Kahlua, fresh cream (shaken, cocktail glass).

Wine Cooler: red wine, 7-Up (10-ounce wine glass).

Yellow Jacket: bourbon, orange juice (highball glass).

Bar Mixology

How to Use the Shaker

Step 1: *Place ice cubes in mixing glass.*

Step 2: *Add drink ingredients.*

Step 3: *Place cup over mixing glass and shake.*

Step 4: *Remove cup and pour into glass.*

Step 5: *Add garnish and stir stick.*

How to Prepare a Drink in a Blender

Step 1: *Place ice cubes in blender cup.*   **Step 2:** *Add drink ingredients.*   **Step 3:** *Blend for several seconds.*

Step 4: *Change cup for strainer and pour in chilled serving glass.*   **Step 5:** *Add garnish and stir stick.*

How to Prepare a Highball

Step 1: *Place ice in glass using scoop.*

Step 2: *Add liquor.*

Step 3: *Add mix to within one inch of rim.*

Step 4: *Stir with bar spoon.*

Step 5: *Add garnish and straw or stir stick.*

How to Prepare a Two-Liquor Drink on the Rocks

Step 1: *Place ice cubes in serving glass.*

Step 2: *Add liquors.*

Step 3: *Stir with bar spoon.*

Step 4: *Add garnish and stir stick or straw.*

How to Prepare a Pousse-Café

Step 1: *Place mixing spoon against side of serving glass.*

Step 2: *Carefully pour layers of liqueur over the back of the spoon, from densest to lightest. Do not stir.*

English	French	Spanish
About	Environ	Alrededor de
Account	Acompte	Cuenta
Acid	Acide	Ácido
Alive	Vif	Vivo
Almond	Amande	Almendra
Anchovy	Anchois	Anchoa
Anniversary	Anniversaire	Aniversario
Announce	Annoncer	Anunciar
Appetite	Appétit	Apetito
Apple	Pomme	Manzana
Apricot	Abricot	Albaricoque
Apron	Tablier	Delantal
Armchair	Fauteuil	Sillón
Aroma	Arôme	Aroma
Aromatic	Aromatique	Aromático
Artichoke	Artichaut	Alcachofa
Ashes	Cendres	Cenizas
Asparagus	Asperges	Espárragos
Back	Dos	Espalda
Bad	Mauvais	Malo

English	French	Spanish
Barbel	Barbeau	Barbo
Barley	Orge	Cebada
Barrel	Barrique	Barril
Basket	Corbeille	Cesta
Bass	Bar	Mero
Bean	Haricot	Habichuela
Bear	Ours	Oso
Bed	Lit	Cama
Beef	Boeuf	Ternera
Beer	Bière	Cerveza
Beetroot	Betterave	Remolacha
Better	Meilleur	Mejor
Bilberry	Myrtille	Arándano
Bill	Addition	Cuenta
Bird	Oiseau	Pájaro
Bitter	Amer	Amargo
Black	Noir	Negro
Blackberry	Mure	Mora
Black currant	Cassis	Casis
Black pudding	Boudin	Morcilla
Blanch	Blanchir	Blanquear
Blood	Sang	Sangre
Boil	Cuire	Cocer
Boiled	Bouilli	Cocido
Bone	Os	Hueso
Bottle	Bouteille	Botella
Box	Boîte	Caja
Brain	Cervelle	Sesos
Braised	Braisé	Braseado
Bread	Pain	Pan
Bread-crumbed	Pané	Empanado

English	French	Spanish
Bread crumbs	Chapelure	Pan rallado
Bream	Brème	Brema
Breast	Poitrine	Pecho
Brill	Barbue	Rodaballo
Broad bean	Fève	Haba
Broth	Bouillon	Caldo
Brown sugar	Cassonade	Azúcar morena
Burn	Brûler	Quemar
Butter	Beurre	Mantequilla
Buy	Acheter	Comprar
Buyer	Acheteur	Comprador
Cabbage	Chou	Col
Cake	Gâteau	Pastel
Camomile	Camomille	Camomila
Cancel	Décommander	Cancelar
Candle	chandelle	Vela
Candle holder	chandelier	Candelabro
Capon	Chapon	Capón
Car	Voiture	Coche
Caraway	Cumin	Comino
Carnation	Oeillet	Clavel
Carp	Carpe	Carpa
Carpenter	Menuisier	Carpintero
Carpet	Tapis	Alfombra
Carrot	Carotte	Zanahoria
Carve	Découper	Trinchar
Cash	Comptant	Efectivo
Castle	Château	Castillo
Cauliflower	Chou-fleur	Coliflor
Cayenne pepper	Cayenne	Cayena

English	French	Spanish
Ceiling	Plafond	Techo
Celery	Céleri	Apio
Cellar	Cave	Cava
Chair	Chaise	Silla
Change	Change	Cambio
Cheese	Fromage	Queso
Cherry	Cerise	Cereza
Chervil	Cerfeuil	Perifollo
Chestnut	Châtaigne	Castaña
Chicken	Poulet	Pollo
China	Porcelaine	Vajilla
Chives	Ciboulette	Cebollino
Choice	Choix	Selección
Chop	Concasser	Picar
Christmas	Noël	Navidad
Cider	Cidre	Sidra
Cinnamon	Cannelle	Canela
Clam	Clovisse	Almeja
Clarify	Clarifier	Clarificar
Clean	Nettoyer	Limpiar
Clear	Clair	Claro
Clear soup	Consommé	Consomé
Clove	Clou de girofle	Clavo
Cocoa	Cacao	Cacao
Cod	Cabillaud	Bacalao
Codfish	Morue	Bacalao
Coffee	Café	Café
Coffeepot	Cafetière	Cafetera
Cold	Froid	Frio
Color	Couleur	Color
Common	Commun	Común

English	French	Spanish
Condense	Condenser	Condensar
Confectionery	Confiserie	Repostería
Conger eel	Lotte	Congrio
Cook	Cuisinier	Cocinero
Cooked	Cuit	Cocido
Cooking pot	Marmite	Olla
Cork	Bouchon	Tapón
Corkscrew	Tirebouchon	Sacacorchos
Corn	Maïs	Maiz
Country	Pays	País
Cover	Couvercle	Tapadera
Cover (table set)	Couvert	Cubierto
Cow	Vache	Vaca
Crab	Crabe	Cangrejo
Cranberry	Airelle rouge	Arándano
Crayfish	Écrevisse	Cangrejo de río
Cream	Crème	Crema
Cucumber	Concombre	Pepino
Culinary	Culinaire	Culinario
Cup	Tasse	Taza
Curtain	Rideau	Cortina
Customer	Client	Cliente
Cutlet	Côtelette	Chuleta
Dark	Foncé	Oscuro
Date	Datte	Dátil
Decoration	Décoration	Decoración
Deer	Cerf	Ciervo
Degree	Degré	Grado
Dessert	Dessert	Postre
Digest	Digérer	Digerir

English	French	Spanish
Dining room	Salle à manger	Comedor
Discount	Escompte	Descuento
Dish	Assiette	Plato
Dissolve	Délier	Disolver
Distillation	Distillation	Destilación
Divide	Deviser	Dividir
Doctor	Médecin	Doctor
Dolphin	Dauphin	Delfín
Door	Porte	Puerta
Dorado	Daurade	Dorada
Double	Double	Doble
Dress	Dresser	Aderezar
Drink	Boire	Beber
Drinkable	Buvable	Bebible
Drop	Goutte	Gota
Drunk	Ivre	Borracho
Dry (to)	Essuyer	Secar
Dry	Sec	Seco
Dry wine	Vin sec	Vino seco
Duck	Canard	Pato
Duckling	Caneton	Patito
Ear	Oreille	Oreja
Easter	Pâques	Pascua florida
Easy	Facile	Fácil
Eat	Manger	Comer
Edible	Mangeable	Comestible
Eel	Anguille	Anguila
Egg	Oeuf	Huevo
Egg cup	Coquetier	Huevera
Eggplant	Aubergine	Berenjena

English	**French**	**Spanish**
Egg white	Blanc d'oeuf	Clara de huevo
Egg yolk	Jaune d'oeuf	Yema
Employee	Employé	Empleado
Empty	Vide	Vacío
Enclosed	Inclus	Incluido
Endive	Chicorée	Endivia
Entrée	Entrée	Entrada
Entremets	Entremets	Entremes
Enveloped	Enveloppé	Envuelto
Essence	Extrait	Extracto
Evaporate	Évaporer	Evaporar
Evening	Soir	Tarde
Example	Example	Ejemplo
Excellent	Excellent	Excelente
Excuse	Excuse	Excusa
Exquisite	Extra	Exquisito
False	Faux	Falso
Fan	Éventail	Ventilador
Fashion	Mode	Moda
Fat	Gras	Graso
Father	Père	Padre
Fennel	Fenouil	Hinojo
Ferment	Fermenter	Fermentar
Festival	Fête	Fiesta
Fig	Figue	Higo
Fillet	Filet	Filete
Fill up	Remplir	Llenar
Filter	Filtrer	Filtrar
Fine	Fin	Fino
Fire	Feu	Fuego

English	French	Spanish
Fish	Poisson	Pescado
Fishbone	Arête	Espina
Fish steak	Darne	Rodaja
Flake	Flocon	Copo
Floor (story)	Étage	Piso
Floor	Plancher	Suelo
Flounder	Flet	Rodaballo
Flour	Farine	Harina
Flower	Fleur	Flor
Flower vase	Vase à fleurs	Jarrón
Food	Aliment	Comida
Foot	Pied	Pié
Foreigner	Étranger	Extranjero
Fork	Fourchette	Tenedor
Fragile	Fragile	Frágil
Fraud	Fraude	Fraude
Fresh	Frais	Fresco
Fried egg	Oeuf frit	Huevo frito
Fritters	Beignets	Buñuelos
Frog	Grenouille	Rana
Front desk	Réception	Recepción
Fruit	Fruit	Fruta
Fruit salad	Macédoine de fruits	Macedonia
Fry	Frire	Freir
Full	Plein	Lleno
Funnel	Entonnoir	Embudo
Furnish	Meubler	Amueblar
Gain	Gagner	Ganar

English	**French**	**Spanish**
Game	Gibier	Caza
Garbanzo beans	Pois chiches	Garbanzos
Garden	Jardin	Jardín
Garlic	Ail	Ajo
Garnish	Garniture	Guarnición
Gastronomy	Gastronomie	Gastronomía
Gherkin	Cornichon	Pepinillo
Ginger	Gingembre	Jengibre
Glass	Verre	Vaso
Glove	Gant	Guante
Goat	Chèvre	Cabra
Good	Bon	Bueno
Goose	Oie	Oca
Gooseberry	Groseille verte	Grosella
Goose liver	Foie gras	Foie gras
Gourmet	Gourmet	Gastrónomo
Grain	Grain	Grano
Grandfather	Grand-père	Abuelo
Grandmother	Grand-mère	Abuela
Grapefruit	Pamplemousse	Pomelo
Grated	Râpé	Rallado
Great	Grand	Grande
Green	Vert	Verde
Green beans	Haricots verts	Judías verdes
Green peas	Petit pois	Guisantes
Grilled	Grillé	A la parrilla
Grouse	Coq de bruyère	Urogallo
Guest	Hôte	Huésped
Guinea fowl	Pintade	Pintada

English	French	Spanish
Haddock	Aiglefin	Abadejo
Hake	Colin	Merluza
Half	Moitié	Mitad
Halibut	Flétan	Hipogloso
Ham	Jambon	Jamón
Handful	Poignée	Puñado
Handle	Manche	Mango
Hard-boiled egg	Oeuf dur	Huevo duro
Hare	Lièvre	Liebre
Hash	Hachis	Salpicón
Hazelnut	Noisette	Avellana
Head	Tête	Cabeza
Head cook	Chef de cuisine	Jefe de cocina
Head waiter	Maître d'hôtel	Maitre
Health	Santé	Salud
Healthy	Sain	Sano
Herbal tea	Tisane	Tisana
Herbs	Herbes	Hierbas
Herring	Hareng	Arenque
Hind leg	Gigot	Pierna
Honey	Miel	Miel
Hop	Houblon	Lúpulo
Horseradish	Raifort	Rábano picante
Hot	Chaud	Caliente
Hot plate	Réchaud	Calentador
Hour	Heure	Hora
Humid	Humide	Húmedo
Hunger	Faim	Hambre
Hunter	Chasseur	Cazador

English	French	Spanish
Ice	Glace	Hielo
Ice cream	Glace	Helado
Iced	Glacé	Helado
Illumination	Illumination	Iluminación
Indigestion	Indigestion	Indigestión
Information	Information	Información
Infusion	Infusion	Infusión
Intestines	Intestin	Intestinos
Inventory	Inventaire	Inventario
Jam	Confiture	Confitura
Jelly	Gelée	Jalea
Juice	Jus	Jugo
July	Juillet	Julio
June	Juin	Junio
Juniper berry	Baie de genièvre	Enebrina
Kernel	Noyau	Pepita
Key	Clef	Llave
Kidney	Rognon	Riñón
Kill	Tuer	Matar
King	Roi	Rey
Kitchen	Cuisine	Cocina
Knife	Couteau	Cuchillo
Lady	Madame	Señora
Lake	Lac	Lago
Lamb	Agneau	Cordero
Larded	Piqué	Mechado
Larding-pin	Aiguille	Aguja

English	French	Spanish
Laurel	Laurier	Laurel
Leaf	Feuille	Hoja
Lean	Maigre	Magro
Leek	Poireau	Puerro
Leg of lamb	Gigot d'agneau	Pierna de cordero
Lemon	Citron	Limón
Lemonade	Limonade	Limonada
Lentils	Lentilles	Lentejas
Lettuce	Laitue	Lechuga
Light (to)	Allumer	Encender
Light	Léger	Ligero
Lime tea	Tilleul	Tila
Linen	Linge	Lencería
Liqueur	Liqueur	Licor
Liquid	Liquide	Líquido
Little	Petit	Pequeño
Liver	Foie	Hígado
Lobster	Homard	Langosta
Lock up	Enfermer	Encerrar
Lose	Perdre	Perder
Lost	Perdu	Perdido
Lukewarm	Tiède	Templado
Macerate	Macérer	Macerar
Mackerel	Maquereau	Caballa
Manager	Directeur	Director
Margarine	Margarine	Margarina
Marmalade	Marmelade	Mermelada
Marrow	Moelle	Médula
Marzipan	Massepain	Mazapán

English	French	Spanish
Master key	Passe-partout	Llave maestra
Matches	Allumettes	Cerillas
Meal	Repas	Comida
Measure	Mesure	Medida
Meat	Viande	Carne
Medicine	Médicament	Medicina
Melon	Melon	Melón
Melt	Fondre	Fundir
Menu	Menu	Menú
Merchandise	Marchandise	Mercadería
Message	Message	Mensaje
Middle	Mileu	Medio
Midnight	Minuit	Medianoche
Milk	Lait	Leche
Mill	Moulin	Molino
Minced	Emincé	Desmenuzado
Mineral water	Eau minéral	Agua mineral
Mint	Menthe	Menta
Mirror	Miroir	Espejo
Miss	Mademoiselle	Señorita
Mistake	Erreur	Error
Mixed	Panaché	Mixto
Mixture	Mélange	Mezcla
More	Plus	Más
Mother	Mère	Madre
Mullet	Mulet	Mújol
Mushroom	Champignon	Seta
Mussel	Moule	Mejillón
Mustard	Moutarde	Mostaza
Mutton	Mouton	Carnero

English	French	Spanish
Napkin	Serviette	Servilleta
Natural	Naturel	Natural
Necessary	Nécessaire	Necesario
Neck	Cou	Cuello
Neglect	Négliger	Abandonar
Nerve	Nerf	Nervio
Nest	Nid	Nido
Night	Nuit	Noche
Noodles	Nouilles	Tallarines
Noon	Midi	Mediodía
Notice	Notice	Aviso
Nourishing	Nourrissant	Nutritivo
Number	Nombre	Número
Nut	Noix	Nuez
Nutmeg	Muscade	Nuez moscada
Oats	Avoine	Avena
Odor	Odeur	Olor
Oil	Huile	Aceite
Old	Vieux	Viejo
Omelet	Omelette	Tortilla
Onion	Oignon	Cebolla
Open	Ouvrir	Abrir
Orange	Orange	Naranja
Order	Commande	Pedido
Ordinary	Ordinaire	Ordinario
Oven	Four	Horno
Oxygen	Oxygène	Oxígeno
Oyster	Huître	Ostra
Painting	Tableau	Pintura

English	**French**	**Spanish**
Pair	Paire	Par
Palace	Palais	Palacio
Palm tree	Palmier	Palmera
Pan	Poêle	Sartén
Pancake	Crêpe	Hojuela
Pantry	Gardemanger	Cuarto frio
Pants	Pantalon	Pantalones
Paper	Papier	Papel
Parcel	Paquet	Paquete
Pardon	Pardon	Perdón
Parsley	Persil	Perejil
Partridge	Perdreau	Perdiz
Paste	Pâte	Pasta
Pastry	Pâtisserie	Pastelería
Pastry cook	Pâtissier	Pastelero
Pay	Paie	Paga
Peace	Paix	Paz
Peach	Pêche	Melocotón
Pear	Poire	Pera
Peel	Éplucher	Pelar
Pepper	Poivre	Pimienta
Perch	Perche	Perca
Perfect	Parfait	Perfecto
Pheasant	Faisan	Faisán
Piece	Morceau	Pedazo
Pigeon	Pigeon	Pichón
Pike	Brochet	Lucio
Pill	Pilule	Píldora
Pimiento	Piment	Pimiento
Pineapple	Ananas	Piña
Pistachio	Pistache	Pistacho

English	French	Spanish
Place	Place	Sitio
Play	Jeu	Juego
Pluck	Déplumer	Desplumar
Plum	Prune	Ciruela
Poached egg	Oeuf poché	Huevo escalfado
Pocket	Poche	Bolsillo
Poisoning	Empoisonnement	Envenenamiento
Poisonous	Vénéneux	Venenoso
Polish	Polir	Pulir
Pomegranate	Grenade	Granada
Pork	Porc	Cerdo
Portion	Portion	Porción
Pot	Pot	Olla
Potato	Pomme de terre	Patata
Poultry	Volaille	Aves
Pound	Livre	Libra
Powder	Poudre	Polvo
Prawn	Langoustine	Langostino
Prepare	Apprêter	Preparar
Price	Prix	Precio
Profit	Profit	Beneficio
Prune	Pruneau	Ciruela pasa
Pudding	Pouding	Budín
Pulp	Pulpe	Pulpa
Pumpkin	Potiron	Calabaza
Purchase	Achat	Compra
Pure	Pur	Puro
Quail	Caille	Codorniz
Quality	Qualité	Calidad

English	French	Spanish
Quantity	Quantité	Cantidad
Quince	Coing	Membrillo
Rabbit	Lapin	Conejo
Radish	Radis	Rábano
Raisin	Raisin	Pasa
Rare	Saignant	Poco hecho
Raspberry	Framboise	Frambuesa
Raw	Cru	Crudo
Ready	Prêt	Listo
Rebate	Rabais	Rebaja
Receipt	Acquit	Recibo
Red mullet	Rouget	Salmonete
Reduce	Réduire	Reducir
Refresh	Refraîchir	Refrescar
Registration	Inscription	Registro
Reimbursement	Remboursement	Reembolso
Repeat	Répéter	Repetir
Reservation	Réservation	Reserva
Reserve	Réserve	Reservar
Rest	Repos	Descanso
Return	Retour	Volver
Rhubarb	Rhubarbe	Ruibarbo
Ribbon	Cordon	Cordón
Rice	Riz	Arroz
Rich	Riche	Rico
Ring	Sonner	Llamar
Ripe	Mur	Maduro
River	Rivière	Río
Roasted	Rôti	Asado
Rooster	Coq	Gallo

English	French	Spanish
Root	Racine	Raiz
Rosemary	Romarin	Romero
Saddle	Selle	Lomo
Saffron	Safran	Azafrán
Sage	Sauge	Salvia
Sailor	Matelot	Marinero
Salad	Salade	Ensalada
Salmon	Saumon	Salmón
Salt	Sel	Sal
Sandwich	Sandwich	Sandwich
Sandy	Sableux	Arenoso
Sardine	Sardine	Sardina
Sauce	Sauce	Salsa
Saucer	Soucoupe	Platillo
Sauerkraut	Choucroute	Chucruta
Sausage	saucisse	Salchicha
Scallop	Escalope	Escalope
Scum	Écume	Espuma
Sea	Mer	Mar
Sea bream	Dorade	Besugo
Season	Saison	Estación
Season (to)	Epicer	Condimentar
Seasoning	Condiment	Condimento
Selection	Assortiment	Selección
Sell	Vendre	Vender
Semolina	Semoule	Sémola
Separate	Séparer	Separar
Shake	Agiter	Agitar
Shark	Requin	Tiburón
Sharp	Âpre	Áspero

English	French	Spanish
Shell	Coquille	Concha
Shellfish	Coquillage	Marisco
Shoe	Soulier	Zapato
Shoulder	Épaule	Espalda
Shrimp	Crevette	Camarón
Shut	Fermer	Cerrar
Sieve	Passoire	Tamiz
Signature	Signature	Firma
Silverware	Argenterie	Vajilla
Simmer	Mijoter	Cocer a fuego lento
Simple	Simple	Simple
Sirloin	Aloyau	Solomillo
Sirloin steak	Entrecôte	Bistec
Skate	Raie	Raya
Skewer	Brochette	Espetón
Skin	Peau	Piel
Sleep	Sommeil	Sueño
Slice	Tranche	Rebanada
Smelt	Éperlan	Eperlano
Smoke	Fumer	Fumar
Smoked	Fumé	Ahumado
Snail	Escargot	Caracol
Snipe	Bécassine	Agachadiza
Snow	Neige	Nieve
Soak	Tremper	Empapar
Soap	Savon	Jabón
Soft	Mollet	Blando
Sole	Sole	Lenguado
Sorrel	Oseille	Acedera
Soup	Soup	Sopa

English	**French**	**Spanish**
Soup tureen	Soupière	Sopera
Sour	Aigre	Agrio
Souvenir	Souvenir	Recuerdo
Sparkling	Mousseaux	Espumante
Sparkling wine	Vin mousseux	Vino espumante
Speak	Parler	Hablar
Spice	Épice	Especia
Spicy	Piquant	Picante
Spinach	Épinard	Espinaca
Spit	Broche	Asador
Spoil	Gâter	Echar a perder
Sponge	Éponge	Esponja
Spoon	Cuillère	Cuchara
Spot	Tâche	Mancha
Staircase	Escalier	Escalera
Starch	Amidon	Almidón
Stay	Séjour	Estancia
Steam	Vapeur	Vapor
Stewed	Étuvé	Estofado
Stewed fruit	Compote	Compota
Stomach	Estomac	Estómago
Straw	Chalumeau	Paja
Strawberry	Fraise	Fresa
String	Ficelle	Bramante
Strong	Fort	Fuerte
Stuffing	Farce	Relleno
Sturgeon	Esturgeon	Esturión
Success	Succès	Éxito
Suckling pig	Cochon de lait	Cochinillo
Sugar	Sucre	Azúcar
Supper	Souper	Cena

English	**French**	**Spanish**
Surprise	Surprise	Sorpresa
Sweet	Doux	Dulce
Sweeten	Adoucir	Endulzar
Sweetened	Sucré	Azucarado
Sweetness	Douceur	Dulzor
Syrup	Sirop	Jarabe
Table	Table	Mesa
Tablecloth	Nappe	Mantel
Tail	Queue	Rabo
Tangerine	Mandarine	Mandarina
Tarragon	Estragon	Estragón
Taste	Gouter	Probar
Tax	Taxe	Impuesto
Tea	Thé	Té
Teapot	Théière	Tetera
Tender	Tendre	Tierno
Thick	Épais	Espeso
Thirst	Soif	Sed
Thyme	Thym	Tomillo
Time	Temps	Tiempo
Tip	Pourboire	Propina
Toast	Pain grillé	Tostada
Tomato	Tomate	Tomate
Tongue	Langue	Lengua
Toothpick	Curedents	Palillo
Tough	Dur	Duro
Towel	Essuie-main	Toalla
Town hall	Mairie	Ayuntamiento
Trade	Métier	Oficio
Traveler	Voyageur	Viajero

English	French	Spanish
Tray	Plateau	Bandeja
Treacle	Mélasse	Melaza
Trout	Truite	Trucha
Truffle	Truffe	Trufa
Tulip	Tulipe	Tulipán
Tumbler	Gobelet	Vaso
Tunny fish	Thon	Atún
Turkey	Dinde	Pavo
Turnip	Navet	Nabo
Turtle	Tortue	Tortuga
Umbrella	Parapluie	Paraguas
Unable	Incapable	Incapaz
Unacceptable	Inacceptable	Inaceptable
Uncork	Déboucher	Descorchar
Uneatable	Immangeable	Incomible
Vanilla	Vanille	Vainilla
Veal	Veau	Ternera
Vegetables	Légumes	Legumbres
Venison	Chevreuil	Venado
Vine	Vigne	Viña
Vinegar	Vinaigre	Vinagre
Vineyard	Vignoble	Viñedo
Vintage	Vendange	Vendimia
Voyage	Voyage	Viaje
Wafer	Gaufrette	Barquillo
Wages	Salaire	Paga
Waiter	Garçon	Camarero
Wake up	Réveille	Llamada

English	French	Spanish
Warm up	Réchauffer	Calentar
Watch	Montre	Reloj
Water	Eau	Agua
Watercress	Cresson	Berro
Watermelon	Pastèque	Sandía
Wax	Cire	Cera
Weak	Faible	Débil
Wedding	Mariage	Boda
Week	Semaine	Semana
Weight	Peser	Pesar
Well-done	Bien cuit	Bien hecho
Wheat	Froment	Trigo
Whipped cream	Crème fouettée	Crema chantilly
Whiting	Merlan	Pescadilla
Wild	Sauvage	Salvaje
Window	Fenêtre	Ventana
Wine	Vin	Vino
Wine list	Carte des vins	Carta de vinos
Wine waiter	Sommelier	Sommelier
Wing	Aile	Ala
Wing of chicken	Aile de poulet	Ala de pollo
Winter	Hiver	Invierno
Woodcock	Bécasse	Becada
Word	Parole	Palabra
Work	Travail	Trabajo
Write	Écrire	Escribir
Yeast	Levure	Levadura
Yellow	Jaune	Amarillo
Zucchini	Courgette	Calabacín

Service Notes

Service Notes

Service Notes

Service Notes

Service Notes

Service Notes

Service Notes